Alex Chudov

WONDER IN THE UNIVERSE

WHO WE ARE AND WHY WE CAME INTO THIS UNIVERSE

ISBN (Paperback): 978-1-0691545-1-4

To my family
both those who share my days
and those who live on in my memories

CONTENTS

GRATITUDE

In my everyday life, I dedicate much time to gratitude. Here, I express my appreciation to everyone and everything dear to me who has influenced my life, worldview, and life experience and assisted me in writing this book.

I thank my parents, grandparents, and ancestors for giving me life and raising me to be worthy.

I thank my family, my beloved wife, and my children for their patience, support, and love.

I thank my siblings and their families for being by my side and walking along the path of life with me.

I thank my friends for their support, invaluable conversations, and life lessons.

I thank you, Universe, for my life, my unique experience, and your support, guidance, inspiration, and revelations!

And I thank you, dear reader, for your interest in my book, and your precious time, and attention!

I want to thank everyone who helped me with this book. Without you, the world would not have seen these lines.

I thank my beloved wife, Hanna, for her inspiration, support, and assistance in editing the book. Without her literary intuition, you would read a "tangle of my thoughts" instead of this beautiful literary text. Thank you, my love!

I express my deepest gratitude to my beloved daughter, Yeva, for your irreplaceable contribution to the main image on the cover. Your gentle hand, guided by your unwavering search for truth, is forever etched within its essence.

I send my warm thanks to the best neighbor ever. Bernie, thank you for your help with editing the first English version of this book.

PROLOGUE

"Who am I? Why have I come into this life? What is my purpose in the Universe?" I have pondered these questions many times throughout my life. I believe I am not alone in this. I assume that you, too, occasionally contemplate these questions. The curiosity inherent in our minds generates many questions about our existence, answers to which not everyone finds.

In this book, I will share my thoughts, ideas, and vision of the processes in the Universe, and I will bear my soul. In part, these are also my memoirs. Please keep your mind open, embrace new information, and always embrace these with common sense and constructive criticism. You will unveil the curtain of the Universe's mysteries, discover food for thought, and sow the seeds of curiosity so that after reading this book, you will ask deeper questions and seek accurate answers.

This book emerged as my response to these questions. It contains the wisdom I have drawn from various sources of information, my life experience, and my vision of the Universe. This vision was finally shaped after an extraordinary experience I went through. This experience was a turning point in my life, dividing it into "before and after."

When my understanding of the Universe's workings and my place in it solidified, I thought it would be wonderful to pass on this knowledge to my children, family, friends, and all those seeking answers. The idea of writing a book came naturally. It is an excellent way to organize my thoughts and preserve them in an easily understandable form for future generations.

I have been incredibly fortunate to experience many life events that have changed my perspective, taught me life wisdom, and allowed me to experience a full spectrum of emotions. My parents, siblings, grandparents, my beloved wife and our children, our friends, life on two continents, in three countries, in five cities, frequent relocations, challenging life situations, a variety of jobs in different fields, a special relationship with religion, escaping war twice, a severe illness, and the battle for life— all of these have formed the foundation of my worldview. All the ideas in this book are based on this worldview, my personal experience, and the knowledge accumulated by humanity over millennia.

After reading this book, you will discover what the Universe and your inner world are made of. You will understand how we interact and the unique relationships within your family and with your friends. You will grasp the place your soul and body hold in this world. You will learn to interact with the Universe in the right way and obtain the desired blessings. Most importantly, armed with this knowledge, you can live a long, happy life filled with love, success, wealth, and everything your soul desires. Consider this book as a "manual for your happy life."

Why do I believe that all of this will work for you? Because I live by these principles. I follow these rules myself. I live and breathe these ideas and wisdom. I am a living embodiment and proof of the examples and opinions in this book. Life has often forced me to make essential choices, adapt to new circumstances, emerge victorious from challenging situations, and adapt to new surroundings. I have faced all life's trials with honor and dignity, and I teach this to my children. If it works for me, it will work for you. The key is to open your mind wider!

After reading this book, you will discover a new world full of wonders, magical transformations, and unique adventures. You will no longer be able to look at the world similarly. New facets of the Universe within and around you will be revealed. And you will find the meaning of your existence and your place in the Universe.

You could postpone reading this book to "better times" or acquire this experience alone. It is entirely possible! I spent about forty years reading hundreds of books, living through thousands of life events, having a near-death experience, and undergoing a consciousness rebirth to acquire this knowledge. It was a magnificent journey! It is worth going through all of it! But do you have those extra forty years? Spending a few evenings reading my book and living the next forty years with a more conscious and happier life is better.

If you are ready for this adventure, keep your mind open and think critically, but wait to dismiss new thoughts and ideas. Give them time to settle in and a chance to manifest themselves. Sow the seeds of new knowledge, let them grow, and reap the rewards. We will walk this path together. I will be right there with you. Let's embark on this journey into the fantastic world of your Universe together! And we will start this journey with the first step—the "foundation" of understanding the Universe.

I await you eagerly. Turn the page quickly, and bon voyage!

MATTER - INFORMATION - MEASURE

"At the core of understanding the Universe lies the ability of our brains to generate measures."

At the foundation of understanding the Universe, there are three simple concepts: MATTER, INFORMATION, and MEASURE. These essential tools will help you find answers to questions, comprehend everything you need, and discover what you seek.

Matter – is what the entire Universe is made of and everything that surrounds us. Galaxies, solar systems, planets, Earth, everything that exists and lives on these planets, everything that surrounds you, all the periodic table elements, molecules, atoms, and so on. Think of matter as the material from which the entire Universe is created.

Information – encompasses everything that can be known about a specific matter. It is all the knowledge that describes Matter and is stored within it.

Measure – is the tool through which we can obtain the necessary information about a specific matter. It is how we understand and describe the world around us.

Let me provide a simple example. Take any ordinary object within your reach, like a spoon you use for eating. The spoon itself is a part of MATTER. Hold it in your hand. Feel its weight, shape, and structure. What can you say about it? What INFORMATION can you obtain about the spoon? To extract information, start applying familiar MEASURES. What is the measurement of the spoon's length? Is it 15 centimeters? Less? Great, you have your first piece of information about this matter. What is the measure of the spoon's color? Is it gray, brown, or white? What is the measure of the spoon's material? Is it metal, wood, or plastic? What is the measure of the spoon's volume? What is the measure of its elasticity? What is the measure of its chemical composition, molecular structure, atomic...? Answers to all these questions will provide you with the necessary information.

We obtain ALL the necessary INFORMATION about specific MATTER by applying different MEASURES.

It's essential to understand that *a part of the matter we are considering contains ALL the necessary information about itself. The question is only which measure we apply to obtain information and understand the matter being studied.*

And why is it a spoon and not a fork, for example? Our measure of shapes tells us that it's a spoon. And why the name "spoon"? Because the language I'm writing has such a concept (measure) applicable to this type and form of matter.

Moreover, it's essential to realize that not all measures are correct. You will often encounter measures that contradict each other. Your task is to develop as universal measures as possible to help you describe the matter around you in a way others can understand.

In the Bible, after the world's creation, it is said that "...and Adam gave names to all cattle, and to the fowl of the air, and to every beast of the field..." Thus, according to the Bible, the first language and words (primary measures) denoting everything that exists were born. The Bible is also one of the measures describing the Universe. Throughout evolution, humanity generates new and new measures. This is the foundational process of understanding the Universe.

I often refer to these three fundamental concepts in this book: matter, information, and measure. May they become new measures of your comprehension of the Universe as well!

STRUCTURE OF THE UNIVERSE

“

"Understanding a structure of the Universe opens the doors to the boundless resources of the Universe."

”

Now that you have the foundation of essential tools: matter, information, and measure, let's attempt to outline and comprehend the structure of the Universe and our place within it.

To understand the Universe and how it interacts with us, I have devised a fundamental diagram called the "structure of the Universe." It matured in my thoughts during the process of my "revelation." I will describe this process and my personal experience later in a separate chapter.

Let's briefly examine the scheme and go through the key concepts. In subsequent chapters, we will expand our understanding of these concepts individually.

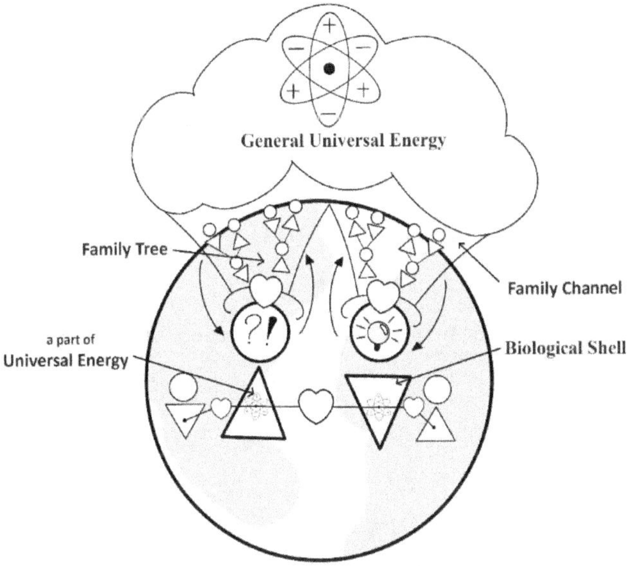

The Structure of the Universe

If we look at it in a very generalized way, the Universe consists of *Universal Energy* and *Universal Matter*. They are like the soul and body of the Universe.

Since humans are "created in the image and likeness of God," we also have a material, biological shell - our body - and a part of Universal Energy commonly known as the "Soul."

Our brain is the most crucial part of our biological shell. *The brain* is an energy center through which Universal Energy interacts with our individual inner energy, our soul. And thus, it interacts with the matter of the surrounding world through us. The brain gathers information about matter through various measures and five senses: sight, hearing, touch, smell, and taste. It then processes this information, comprehends it, stores it, and uses it for interaction and modification.

An essential element in the interaction between humans and Universal Energy is the "*Family Tree*" and the "*Family Channel.*" The Family Tree is a gathering of Universal Energy particles released from the biological shells of people who lived in your family before. In other words, it comprises the souls of people from your family who have "passed into the better world." The Family Tree is the most potent aggregation of Universal Energy, best suited for your interaction with the Universe. The Family Channel is the sheath around the Family Tree that concentrates its energy and facilitates your "connection" to Universal Energy.

We need a force capable of attracting these energies to facilitate the interaction between our soul, inner energy, and Universal Energy through the brain and the Family Tree. That force is *Love.* "pure nonconditional Love" - the most potent of emotions - opens the door to the Universe.

Interaction with the Universe is used for gratitude, making requests to the Universe, receiving guidance and answers to our questions, and for moments of revelation and enlightenment.

For you, these still need to be more specific concepts that only loosely sketch the details of the complete picture. For now, the most important thing is to see the whole picture. Take another look at the diagram, and let's explore the intricacies of Universe Creation and our role in it together.

UNIVERSAL ENERGY AND MATTER

"The Universe, like all living things within it, has its flesh and soul."

Universal Matter is a hypothetical substance from which absolutely everything in the Universe is made of atoms, molecules, and cells within us, our biological shell, various types of plants, numerous animals, raging seas and oceans, vast land, mighty mountains, and the boundless sky, the planets of the Solar System, our Galaxy, and other galaxies. All this matter is tangible to some extent. It would be best to find a way to "touch" it.

In most Universal Matter, "Life" is absent. Universal Energy breathes Life into this Matter. It can also be referred to as the "Energy of Life." This energy is the "Soul" of the Universe. It permeates Matter with an invisible thread and animates it so that parts of this Universal Matter interact with each other, change, and form new varieties.

Universal Energy cannot directly interact with any matter. For example, it cannot move a stone, pick up your spoon from the table, or turn this page. Universal Energy uses other forms of matter with Life Energy inside for interactions—for instance, humans or animals. An elephant is a living being. Its particle of Universal Energy - its soul - animates its body's biological matter, allowing it to interact with other forms of matter. An elephant can move a stone that Universal Energy cannot touch directly, but an inanimate stone, in turn, cannot move the elephant.

Through "living matter with Life Energy inside," Universal Energy can explore and interact with many other types of matter, including humans. Thus, the Universe gains knowledge about itself and evolves.

It's essential to understand that the independent particles of Universal Energy, which breathe Life into biological shells, are no longer entirely controlled by the Universe. These living particles have a unique gift from the moment of their birth. They can grow and develop, make decisions independently, and interact with the world around them using various measures and their biological shell. The Universe experiments with different types of matter through these particles and transforms them into something new.

Although Universal Energy does not have complete control over its "free particles," the connection between them remains. We can communicate with the Universe, and it can respond to us. Leaving clues and clear signs, answering our "prayers," and rewarding us with revelations and enlightenment, the Universe can guide Life in the right direction, thus continuing to evolve.

Understanding Universal Energy also involves the realization that it is not homogeneous. It is simultaneously "positive" and "negative." These two types of Energy are known by various names in world cultures: Yin and Yang, black and white, good and evil, and so on.

If you were to imagine all Universal Energy as a sphere, you would not see two distinct halves of this energy - one negative and one positive. Instead, it would appear as if these two energies had mixed and formed a single "General Universal Energy." This means that there are no extremes in the charge of Universal Energy. The Universe cannot be 100% positive or negative.

A human cannot be 100% "positive" - good, loving, caring, or 100% "negative" - evil, greedy, hating everything and everyone, similarly, with Universal Energy. It shifts between states, depending on the type of matter it interacts with and the processes happening within it. The Universe is in a constant process of energy transitioning from one state to another, which entails alternating processes of creation and destruction.

The Universe seeks to balance between the "positive" and "negative" states in search of harmony. It's important not to think of "negative energy" as a Universal evil. No, it's the Universe's way of balancing and recreating something anew. It's impossible to build a world that is 100% good. The Universe sometimes chooses a different path, and so does humanity. Sometimes, to set the Universe back on its intended development course, you must "break the old to build something new." Destruction in the name of creation.

It's also essential to understand that Universal Energy grows and evolves like a living organism. The growth of this energy is ensured by the development of energy inside living organisms. When an organism is born, a tiny energy particle detaches from General Universal Energy. This newly born particle is "the Spark of Life." As the organism matures and interacts with the Universe, this Spark increases within the biological shell. After death, it is released and reunites with General Universal Energy again, but in a larger quantity than initially. This is how Life in the Universe continues to develop and thrive.

By now, you may have questions about what else Universal Energy resembles, what other names it goes by, and how else people describe it. This Universal Energy is something inexplicably greater than us, powerful, existing beyond our comprehension, capable of creating everything around us and governing this world. Your suspicions are correct! This is what people call God, Allah, Buddha, and so on.

As humans, we are like a miniature projection of the Universe, like a cell in its organism. Inside our matter, Universal Energy resides, governing this matter. To answer the question "Who are we?" let's start by getting acquainted with our biological shell. We'll examine it in more detail in the next chapter.

THE BIOLOGICAL SHELL OF HUMANITY

“

"Our biological shell is like a miniature Universe, full of life and energy within."

”

The human body serves as the biological shell for our particle of Universal Energy, our Soul. The body is a material casing through which the Soul interacts with the world, extracts and studies information from it, and alters its matter.

While unable to directly interact with certain types of matter, the Universe has created various biological shells with fragments of its energy through millennia of evolution. These shells mutated and transformed, accommodating increasing energy and introducing greater diversity in how Universal Energy and Matter interacted.

Plants and animals spread across the Earth, fish populated the seas and oceans, birds conquered the skies, and humans ventured into space. This process of evolution has existed, still exists, and will continue, with or without us. For now, the universal experiment's pinnacle is the human's biological shell. Our body has become a versatile vessel for the Soul, enabling us to interact with the world on an unprecedented scale.

Indeed, like all living beings in the Universe, we possess what is known as *Genetically Determined Potential.* It establishes certain genetic boundaries that the body cannot exceed. "One born to crawl cannot fly."

For example, if you were to wish to soar into the sky like a bird or dive deep underwater like a fish, you would only succeed with additional equipment. Our biological shell has physiological limitations encoded in our DNA.

Everyone possesses a unique set of these genetically determined potentials. Some are born with vocal cords that enable them to sing opera. Some have towering heights, destined to be athletes. And others possess innate oratorical talent, motivating people to accomplish remarkable feats.

It doesn't matter who you are—a musician, an artist, a chef, a skilled builder, or a caring mother. The crucial task for each of us is to recognize and understand our genetically determined potential. This allows us to utilize it and gain a new experience of interacting with the surrounding world. This makes the process of understanding the matter through Universal Energy more productive.

Sometimes, particularly distinctive parts of genetic potential are called a "Gift from God," and various sacred texts emphasize that it should not be squandered. This is true. It should be used if the Universe has granted you a unique gene! Develop your talents: write books, paint pictures, sing songs, engage in sports. This invaluable experience propels the Universe towards discoveries and transformations.

To those who feel they lack a "Gift from God," I say the following. Besides your genetically determined potential, you can acquire and develop other talents. Often, received skills that you diligently cultivate can shine brighter than the "Gift from God" that remains unused or underdeveloped.

An important note: Unlike plants and animals, our biological shell is endowed with an incredible tool — our developed brain. It can be self-awareness, abstract thinking, idea generation, and endless innovation for extracting information from matter. Our brain allows us to step beyond the limits of genetically determined potential. We have learned to create something new and extraordinary from various materials. This has enabled us to fly in the sky, swim underwater, move swiftly on land, and venture into the boundless cosmos.

Even more important than developing your potential is caring for your biological shell. I won't delve into the importance of a healthy lifestyle, proper sleep, exercise, and nutrition here. Countless books have been written, videos produced, and movies have been made on this subject. People of our time are paying more attention to this aspect of life and taking better care of their bodies. This is a splendid trend!

I only want to emphasize the profound significance of caring for your body. Many people know this, but not everyone fully grasp it. You have precisely ONE body in this life, and there won't be another. From birth to death, you have an indefinite number of years allotted to you. How many of those years you have largely depends on you. It depends on your lifestyle, your diet, your physical activity, and how you spend your time.

The biological shell is given to your Soul to achieve the most efficient interaction with the material part of the Universe. The healthier your body, the more productive and longer your life will be. This means your Soul can experience new things and grow to its maximum potential. That very "spiritual growth" is an increase in the volume of Universal Energy within your body.

Remember, your life experience is unique! There won't be another one exactly like it. You have only this one amazing life! It must be cherished and lived to its fullest. Your biological shell is the key to understanding the world for the Universe.

Let's discuss the differences in our biological shells. For many people, these differences become stumbling blocks, reasons for mockery, ridicule, or discrimination based on race. This wrong attitude toward external differences among people needs to be eradicated to reduce anger and hatred on our planet.

A person's skin is like a "biological costume" that, along with our "mask," our face, we wear to the ball called "Life." The Universe has created a vast array of these human costumes and masks. Countless races and ethnicities inhabit our planet. You can encounter someone who looks different from you in every corner of the Earth.

And if someone thinks that the skin of their "compatriots" and their skin is a valid reason for aggression and intolerance toward others, I will ask you to take a closer look at your surroundings. How similar are you to the people in your city? At work? At home? Besides your skin, what sets you apart? Are you as like your neighbor, colleague, or even your parents as you think? The answer is one: You all differ from each other! You are one of a kind on Earth! Even with your parents, you are only partially alike. And since everyone around you differs, should aggression be directed towards them, too, just because they are "different from you"?

The same goes for all people on Earth. We are all unique and different from one another. And this is not a reason for negative attitudes toward each other. The Universe has created many colors for our biological costumes and masks, but we are all one biological species—Homo Sapiens (Thinking Human). We are all human! Humanity is a single biological species! We are a commonality, both biologically and spiritually.

If you still believe that the differences in our biological shells are a reason for displaying negative emotions, then conduct the following mental experiment. Imagine yourself and a person standing before you without biological costumes or skin. What will you see? Muscles, tendons, ligaments, and so on. In both you and the other person, they will be the same. Do you now differ significantly from each other?

If it's hard to imagine, look at a biology textbook in the "human anatomy" section, and lo and behold! You will find only ONE image depicting the structure of human muscles for the ENTIRE Homo Sapiens species! The only thing that distinguishes us from one another is the outer layer—our biological costume. Now, imagine yourself in a different-colored biological outfit. Do you differ significantly on the inside now?

All right, you might say, but the shapes of our faces—our masks—differ significantly. We have different nose shapes, eye shapes, lips, ears, eyebrows, etc. Yes, you are right. But is that a reason to "point out differences"? These distinctions help make us unique! Imagine what our world would look like if everyone on Earth looked precisely the same, like two peas in a pod.

Think about it. Down Syndrome is merely an additional chromosome to the existing 46, acquired through genetic mutations. Just one chromosome! This mutation alters a person's face so that all individuals with this 47th chromosome resemble each other. They look alike regardless of race, skin color, or family affiliation. Ponder this! Just ONE chromosome creates external similarities among people. Are these now essential differences in our masks?

The Universe created the differences in our biological shells and masks to help us better adapt to different survival conditions. It enables us to gain new experiences interacting with matter in all corners of our planet and, in the future, beyond. Darker skin helps people adapt more quickly to the hottest corners of the Earth. Unique eye structures make it easier to endure strong winds and dust. Our special features are the key to survival in the harsh conditions of life on our planet.

Stop thinking negatively about other people solely because of visible differences! Humanity is a single species! We all wear different "biological clothing."

Be more tolerant toward each other; this will eradicate anger, discord, and wars on Earth. Look, for example, in Canada and the people living there. This multicultural country is home to dozens of different nations. All these people are tolerant of each other. They live, work, and thrive in one land, one state. Canada is like "Noah's Ark of Humanity," where "everyone finds a pair."

Walking the streets of major metropolises, small towns, and villages, you will meet people of almost all nationalities and religions and hear many languages from around the world. The only thing that unites them externally is their smile! And what allows them all to live in peace and harmony? Correct, tolerance toward each other and the understanding that we are ALL human, one species, one family. This is an excellent example of the values on which the future of all humanity should be built!

HUMAN ENERGY

"

"Within you lies an energy capable of changing the Universe."

"

The Human Soul is a fragment of the General Universal Energy (see the diagram "The Structure of the Universe") placed within our biological shell. We are "made in the image and likeness" of the Universe. Consequently, like the Universe, we consist of matter and the energy that gives this matter Life.

Your inner energy is both positive and negative simultaneously. Depending on your life experiences and emotions (happiness, love, faith, hope, anger, hatred), you will charge and nourish one type of energy over the other. There is no pure, 100% negative or positive energy. These types of energy coexist within you, intermingling with each other. Life circumstances will always nourish you with energies of different polarities. Try to become entirely righteous or the embodiment of pure evil, and you will realize that this task is unattainable. Yet, this is the foundation of our inner harmony – our balance of "Yin and Yang." Yes, indeed. What lies at the core of the concepts of Yin and Yang in Eastern cultures is the essence of our Universe and our soul as a part of Universal Energy.

Our inner human energy, our Soul, is genderless. However, the biological shell can be male or female. Through interaction with the world, they provide us with different life experiences. This is another way the Universe lives and experiences various interactions with its matter.

The journey of our Soul begins with the process of forming a child in a mother's womb. Part of the genetic material from the mother and father is passed on to the child to create a new gene pool, a new set of DNA. Thus, the experiment of perfecting the biological form called "evolution" continues. At the same time, the Soul "attaches" itself to the embryo's biological shell at an early stage. Where does this fragment of the Soul, this "spark of life," come from? It originates from General Universal Energy. A small portion of energy separates to start a new life, evolving and growing within the individual throughout their life.

The cycle of life begins with the "Spark of Life" inside the human shell. Throughout one's life, a person accumulates and increases the energy within. This energy is released after the body's death. Through the most vital connection – nonconditional love, our soul is drawn to the souls of our ancestors who passed away earlier and became a part of the Family Tree.

My grandmother once said, "A person lives as long as they are remembered." This became my initial vague concept of the Family Tree. Later, I understood that our memories and love for them bind the souls of our parents, grandparents, and other ancestors. If we remember them and express gratitude, their souls remain a part of the Family Tree, infusing it with strength. The stronger your Family Tree, the more powerful your connection to the Universe.

Naturally, many of us only remember or know some of our ancestors from many generations ago. What happens to the souls of ancestors whose memory is lost? Their energetic connection to the Family Tree weakens, and eventually, their energy is released and becomes part of the General Universal Energy.

The fragments of energy that were more positively charged, meaning they lived happier lives, are attracted to the positive aspect of Universal Energy. In contrast, negatively charged pieces are drawn to the negative. However, the Universal Energy remains an indivisible whole. Just like within us, it balances and seeks harmony.

When a new living organism is conceived, the Spark of Life ignites within it. This tiny energy fragment separates from the General Universal Energy and connects with a new biological shell. This newly created Spark of Life contains positive and negative energy types. The embryo's body becomes a vessel for the Soul in this incarnation. This is how Life is born in a new body, and the Universe continues to increase its energy and evolve.

Upon separating from Universal Energy, a new Soul sometimes maintains a solid connection to the energy from its previous incarnation, from which it detached. This happens because the energy within us is whole and has strong bonds between its fragments. Thanks to the connection to a previous incarnation, we sometimes feel the influence of past lives on us.

I believe you have met people in whom a soul of a different gender resides. Such individuals' life positions and behaviors do not align with our concept of their biological gender. There's no need to condemn these people. Remember, the soul is genderless, but the accumulated experience of past lives can deceive a person's consciousness. They may live in disharmony with their bodies.

There's no catastrophe in this. A person can and should live a happy and fulfilling life in their given time. The Universe's task remains the same: to gain new experiences and information through interactions with matter while maximizing human energy during the lifespan of its biological shell. This is how Universal Energy continues its life cycle.

People with a "different" soul inside their bodies often form couples and families with individuals whose biological shells belong to the same gender. The reason is simple: Love—the most significant force of attraction between two souls. Not everyone can realize and accept such relationships, but that's how the Universe operates. Love draws their souls together.

It's also worth mentioning that the natural creation of new biological shells is interrupted when such couples form. Same-sex couples cannot naturally conceive and bring forth new life.

Consequently, a new fragment of Universal Energy cannot form and develop. If the number of such couples continues to increase, it will become a dead-end branch in the development of humanity and the Universe.

Indeed, the Universe is the wisest experimenter, and through humans, it seeks alternative ways of bringing life into existence. Artificial fertilization, surrogate motherhood, and potential human cloning in the future – all these methods partially address the issue of continuing life. But this is not the natural path! We should contemplate and understand where it might lead.

Another crucial point worth discussing is the life cycle of Universal Energy outside of humans. Souls can be born as small fragments of energy within any living organism. Everywhere there is life: animals, birds, plants, insects, and so on. As the residing organism grows, so does the energy within it, up until its death. In the next life, this particle can be reborn in a different form, requiring more energy and offering the opportunity to experience a new life. In this way, particles of Universal Energy are reborn in new and other forms. If new biological shells are being created, this life cycle is endless. This is Life itself.

FAMILY TREE

"

*"This is the most powerful energetic entity,
when you connect with it, you embrace
the entire Universe."*

"

The "Family Tree" represents the convergence of energies from departed souls of a specific lineage. It's an "energy channel" in an inverted triangular shape. At its base are particles of Universal Energy from the parents. The mother's soul is on the left, and the father's is on the right. Above them are the souls of the grandparents. Each pair of grandparents is connected to their descendants accordingly: the mother's parents on her side, the father's parents on his side. Grandmothers and grandfathers are positioned similarly to parents: women on the left, men on the right. The following "layer" of the Tree consists of the souls of your great-grandmothers and great-grandfathers. This continues until the relatives whose souls still have a connection to the lineage, whom we still remember.

If we don't know or remember certain lineage members, their place in the Family Tree remains "empty." Their soul departs into the General Universal Energy. An incomplete Family Tree continues to function but not as effectively as a complete one. The more relatives we remember, honor their memory, express gratitude, and communicate with them, the stronger our Family Tree becomes. The stronger our lineage!

The thread of Love interconnects all the energy particles of your lineage. The stronger the love during life, the stronger the connection between the souls and the more robust your Family Tree. If there were conflicts, hatred, and discord among relatives, the connection between their souls in the Family Tree would be weak. Such souls forget quickly and release themselves from the Tree, dissolving into the General Universal Energy. Consequently, these "lost souls" cannot nourish your Family Tree and, by extension, you.

The “Family Channel” is the "shell" of your Family Tree. This channel is like a funnel through which Universal Energy flows to you, passing through your Family Tree. Whether your Tree is complete or not, strong or weak, the Family Channel envelops it and provides access to its base through the souls of your parents. You can draw energy from the Tree, communicate with your lineage, and interact with the Universe through it.

To be connected to your Family Tree means to have constant access to Universal Energy. This, in turn, offers boundless opportunities for developing your inner energy and leads to a more productive and fulfilling life.

I have always felt that someone is looking out for me, providing guidance and holding my hand through life. I've found dozens of confirmations for this, and I used to think of them as my "Guardian Angels." Then, the idea crept in that my grandmothers were watching over me. Now, I know it's my Family Tree behind it all. My parents and grandparents lead, protect, and guide me on this challenging path called Life.

***

The Family Tree is just one of many *energetic channels* connected to General Universal Energy. If you are aware of the existence of the Family Tree and learn to use it correctly, it becomes the most potent energetic channel for you. Most importantly, it becomes your channel to the Universe.

The rest of these energetic channels have been given different names (measures) by humanity: egregors, collective consciousness, the information field, and so on. But they all share the same essence: they are energetic flows into the Universe, fueled by the energy of the person who connects to them.

Examples of such channels include religions, wars, governments and nations, social media, consuming negative news, etc. In general, anything that grabs our attention and depletes our energy.

Strong emotions connect a person to various energetic channels. Not only can love to establish a strong link between the particles of Universal Energy, but other emotions can do so to a lesser extent. Happiness, excitement, fear, hatred, and any intense emotion can generate an energetic surge that connects you to a channel.

Any energetic channel takes your energy and attention. Do you watch negative news all day long? You're expending energy. Do you live someone else's life on social media? That's energy depletion. Constantly engage in conflicts with others? Get entangled in the wrong crowd? Fanatically defend your political idol? Attend religious institutions? All of this consumes your inner energy.

Like everything in the Universe, these channels can be positive or negative. How do you discern which type of energy they belong to? It's pretty simple. What emotion do you feel while connected to the channel? Is it fear, anger, laughter, or joy? The type of the entire energy channel depends on the charge of the emotion.

It's important to understand that your time and energy are not infinite. It's up to you to choose which energetic channels to connect to. My life experience shows that you shouldn't scatter your attention and should learn to focus on positive energy channels, especially your family's Family Tree.

* * *

I want to draw special attention to "political" and "religious" energy channels. Both are powerful in our time. And for the most part, it is because of them that conflicts, disagreements, discord, and wars occur among humanity.

With political channels, things are relatively straightforward. Throughout the history of humanity, people have created numerous languages, nationalities, and traditions - many measures set us apart. Since different nations used measures that were incomprehensible to each other, conflicts and wars began to arise. Pursuing material values such as wealth, land, and intangible ones like power contributed to this. Thus, humanity has been living from one war to another for thousands of years, redistributing matter and energy over it.

Our familiar planet, Earth, shared by all living beings, is divided by human-made borders of countries, cities, and regions. We've built fences and separated ourselves from others to possess a piece of land its natural resources, and control all of it.

Political channels constantly attract our attention and feed on our energy. Some people "heroically" engage in political battles while sitting on the couch. Others, strong-willed, participate in rallies and protests. And some sacrifice their lives in wars, defending what they hold dear.

But if we try to abstract ourselves from political channels, what, for example, would happen if we removed all the borders of countries? What would remain? Look at the geographical map of the world. You can draw imaginary country borders on it as much as you want, erase them, and draw them again. What would this change for the planet as a whole? Nothing.

Countries' borders are our historical legacy. But it is possible to live without them. Undoubtedly, this is a process that takes time. It can take decades, centuries, or even millennia. But humanity, as a unified species, will establish a common form of governance and a suitable territory on Earth. When people realize that we are not different nations, but we are one form of life - Earthlings. Then, the common interests of the survival of all humanity and all life in the Universe will become more critical than territorial division and resources. And then our energy will be redirected to more beneficial energy channels than political ones.

Indeed, in forming a Unified Human Race, we must remember our national and cultural differences. This is our heritage and the diverse experience of the Universe that we need to cherish and develop together. Today, hundreds of nations and cultures coexist in one country, such as Canada. They continue to honor the memory of their ancestors, customs, songs, stories, national clothing, and food, but at the same time, they are inclined to be peaceful towards other nations. People of different nationalities learn about the cultural traditions of other peoples, adopt their experiences, and incorporate them into their daily lives. This process of merging different cultures will create a "unified human culture" that will absorb the best of what we have.

Now, let's delve into the essence of "religious" energy channels.

What is religion and God? What is at their core? Any religion is nothing but a measure of the people who sought a way to describe the Universe, its laws, and our place in it. These measures are diverse and manyfold, but the essence is the same: God, Allah, Buddha, and pagan gods - all different names for the General Universal Energy.

Why did the image of God emerge? Humans have a visual way of thinking. It's easier for us to conceive of something if it has an idea. Some use the name "God," while I use the term "Universe." This helps me to abstract a bit from religion because it's not only a description of God but also a set of laws and rules by which humanity has lived for millennia. However, not all religious traditions and regulations align with my worldview.

I encountered certain circumstances in my childhood that I couldn't influence, change, or prevent. And like all people on Earth, I began to "pray." But for me, prayer was never a memorized passage of text, even if it was a beautifully composed verse that could be recited. For me, prayer was always a way to address "God," but in my own words, and most importantly, sincerely, emotionally, and from the heart! In those moments, I noticed that my prayers were heard!

For example, once, I prayed for my older brother, Sergey. The phone rang late at night when everyone was going to bed. Dad picked up the receiver. After a few seconds of conversation, he jumped out of bed and woke Mom. A few minutes later, our parents were getting ready in a hurry and discussing something actively. I don't remember the conversation, but Mom was upset, and Dad tried calming her down. I understood that something serious had happened. Then, Mom rushed into the room where my brother and I lived. I was lying alone in the dark, listening to the adults' conversation. Mom turned on the light. She quickly said, "Your brother was hit by a car. Your father and I need to go to him urgently. Take care of your little sister," she left the room. In a moment, my younger sister Tanya and I were alone in an empty apartment. I don't remember if my sister was sleeping or if she heard everything, but at that moment, I was left alone with my thoughts.

"What happened? Is my brother alive? What will happen now? How will our parents live with this?" Grim thoughts rolled over one after another. A lump formed in my throat, and my eyes began to water. I was scared, confused, and alone in the dark room. Fear gave birth to despair, and all I could do was pray. I tried remembering at least one prayer worth addressing to the Almighty, but I didn't know any. My knowledge of religion then boiled down to the ability to cross myself, and not always correctly.

Desperate, I began asking God for help in my words and chaotic thoughts. I lay in the darkness. I couldn't hear sounds feel the sheets, blankets, or even the bed itself. It was as if everything around had disappeared. I didn't even feel my own body. I was completely immersed in my thoughts: "Lord God, you are all-powerful! I beg you to help my brother survive! My family won't be able to bear such sorrow. I love my brother very much and can't bear to lose him. God, I beg you, help!" I continued to pray until I fell asleep from exhaustion.

I woke up in the middle of the night for just a few minutes. Someone entered the room and turned on a bright light. Oh, a miracle! God had heard my prayers. My brother was alive! He looked scared but appeared physically fine. Only one of his arms was lightly bandaged at the elbow. Our parents had put him to bed. Mom kissed me on the forehead and said, "Everything's okay, my dear." "My brother is alive. Thank you, God!" I thought and fell back asleep with a sense of inner peace.

This story had a happy ending for my brother and us all. It turned out that my brother and his friends had been crossing the road in an unauthorized place at night. The driver of the car, exceeding the speed limit, overlooked Sergey immediately. After the collision with the car, my brother flew a few meters above the ground, somersaulted several times, got up, and walked away as if nothing had happened. Bystanders immediately called the police and an ambulance. During the examination, the medics found only minor wounds on his arm and a tuft of hair torn out, which had lodged in a crack in the car's windshield upon impact. When asked, "How do you feel?", my brother said he was fine, and they let him go. Eventually, the police determined that both parties were at fault. The ambulance was needed for the witness, an older man whose blood pressure skyrocketed from seeing my brother's acrobatics.

This life experience made me understand two important things about God and religion. First, I realized that there is something greater than us and something powerful that hears our prayers and can influence a situation. Yes, I know my brother was fine even without my prayers, but it all seemed like God's plan to me at that moment.

Second, that experience planted a seed of doubt about the process of prayer. "Is it necessary to memorize all these prayers to communicate with God? Which religion's prayers should I choose for this?" These thoughts lingered with me for a long time.

In the following years, in difficult moments, I often turned to God in prayer. I asked for help in my own words and an arbitrary form. And surprisingly, God heard my prayers and helped me. This practical experience reinforced my theory about "the importance of sincerity in any words of prayer, rather than memorizing prayer verses."

At a certain point, the company where my father worked began construction on a church. My dad was one of the few responsible for the project. During that time, he befriended the clergyman appointed as the head of the church. The church was splendid, though small, but beautiful and cozy. Next to the church, they built a house for the clergyman. It was neat, of average size, and well-furnished with religious items and furniture. This house reminded me of a wealthy person's home rather than a modest priest's residence. My father and I often visited this house for various reasons. We also visited the "behind-the-scenes" areas of the church, where the average parishioner rarely set foot. All this allowed me to lift the veil of mystery and religiosity surrounding the church. I understood that clergy members were just people like us. That churches and temples were creations of human hands—buildings constructed by us, not God.

One day, passing by this church, I pondered, "Why do people attend church? Why do they need a special place and another person to communicate with God? Why should we turn to others when we have a power capable of 'connecting us to God directly'? What then is the point of religion and churches?" This moment remains vivid in my memories for over 20 years. I remember it as if it happened yesterday. It marked the beginning of my "personal" and "direct" communication with God and frequent contemplations on the essence of religions.

After many years of contemplation, my measure regarding religions took shape. It may not appeal to everyone, and I do not claim absolute truth in all its manifestations.

It is essential to note that every religion on Earth was not created by "Gods" but by ordinary, living people like you and me. In their time, they, just like other authors, invented and recorded the texts of future great books: the Bible, the Old Testament, the Quran, the Vedas, the Talmud, and so on.

Moses received a "revelation" from God and delivered "10 commandments" to humanity. The text was not extensive but crucial for that era. I believe the prophet received a "revelation" from the Universe and recorded it in commandments. However, with limited understanding and knowledge of the Universe, he assumed that "God" had sent these commandments to him. What matters is that this event occurred. It became pivotal in the formation and establishment of the Christian religion. I will describe my understanding of "revelation" in a separate chapter.

Similarly, all religions were born, flourished, and gained strength. Humans invented and wrote all these books, reflecting new religious rules and laws, thereby shaping new perspectives on the Universe.

The concept of God was created by humanity to make it easier to connect with the Universe. After all, isn't it much simpler to envision the image of a humanoid deity than to grasp the entire Universe in our thoughts? Religion envelops the divine figure with an aura of "omnipotence and mystery" to give worshippers an image that evokes strong emotions. These emotions generate a powerful stream of thoughts to connect our inner energy with the Universe.

All icons, images of saints, and beautiful and majestic architecture of churches and temples are designed to evoke our strongest emotions: admiration, reverence, awe, faith, and nonconditional love! Moreover, inside a church, you feel a sense of unity with the Almighty. During prayer, you seem to detach yourself from the external world, completely immersing yourself in your thoughts. It's challenging to compare church prayer with my communication with God while lying in bed at night. However, it has worked and will continue to work for countless believers worldwide.

As a part of the energy channel, the concept of God often replaces the Family Tree for many. People invented religion and God to have an image of a fragment of energy they could address to connect with the Universe. Many nations worldwide have had and still have orphaned children, blatant hatred for relatives, or simply the absence of family values. What should such people do ? How can they connect with the Universe without a Family Tree ? The answer is one – religion and the image of God. They have the power to awaken the strongest emotions in believers, including love. Thus, faith in God, love for him, and prayer to him can replace the connection to the Family Tree.

I reiterate that if you have a strong connection with your Family Tree, you don't need either religion or gods. You can communicate with the Universe directly without intermediaries ! All you need to do is understand how to make your connection as effective as possible and learn to use it as needed and desired.

Religious energy channels, like political ones, will eventually fade into the background. Consider what will happen if every individual can independently address and interact with the Universe directly. What if all religions and mentions of deities vanish in an instant ? Will life on Earth cease to exist ? It existed long before the emergence of religions and will continue to exist afterward. Moreover, religions are a part of human culture. Do animals, plants, birds, and fish need gods to live and explore the world around them?

I, by no means, advocate for eradicating all religions from our lives! This phenomenon is our cultural heritage! These thoughts, texts, and images carry tremendous benefits for all of humanity. Many people find support, solace, and hope in religion, which will continue for hundreds of years. However, I believe that religions, in their current form, will eventually cease to exist. What's important is that people can transfer the goodness, light, purity, and wisdom they contain into a new format, into new perspectives on the Universe. Part of these new perspectives will be the Family Trees of each of us.

LOVE

> *"Love is the most powerful energetic connection between souls in the Universe."*

As we have already discovered, any strong emotion connects the particles of Universal Energy, our souls. I believe the most potent of these emotions is Love – the most significant force of attraction within the Universe.

Love most often blossoms when two people meet, their gazes meet, and the first words are spoken. This state is described in various ways: "It was like a spark flew," "I felt something for her," and "Something ignited between us." All of this is the state of "being in love," that moment when souls first touch.

During this time, strong emotions are born within our biological shell due to the release of various hormones: oxytocin (tenderness and attachment), endorphin (pleasure and euphoria), and serotonin (happiness). They charge and nourish you energetically. Your soul's vital inner energy allows you to reach out to your "other half." Why the other half? Because your souls intertwine into one energetic knot with the threads of Love.

The state of being in love, accompanied by intense emotions, events, and experiences, varies in duration for different couples. For some, it may be weeks or months, while for others, it may be six months or more. The "honeymoon period" of being in love primarily aims to strengthen your spiritual connection to weave your souls together.

Love must be mutual during this time. Often, one person experiences intense feelings of love while the other may have no more than platonic interest or even reject the admirer. This happens because not all the souls you encounter on your journey will be your "soulmates." We'll discuss them in the next chapter. For now, it's worth noting that if your love is not directed toward a soulmate, you won't experience mutual attraction, and you won't be able to form a strong spiritual connection.

At the same time, your biological shell may continue to produce hormones and nourish you energetically. However, in combination with the absence of mutual love, this will lead to the opposite result. You'll be overwhelmed by disappointment, pain, and hatred. These powerful negative emotions will erode your body poison your soul, and your life.

At such a moment, it's essential to understand that you haven't yet met your soulmate, and this love was not mutual. Then, it will be easier for you to endure the pain of separation and loss. After a certain period, you should continue searching for "the one." You can build a family and live a long and happy life together with them! Remember, in the Universe, your true other half, your true love, will inevitably be found. The key is to keep searching, believing, and asking the Universe for a fateful encounter.

After the initial stage of being in love, when passions cool, hormones subside, and the "rose-colored glasses" come off, you are left alone with the reality of your relationship. Here, the strength of your souls' connection, forged during the initial stages of love, becomes the foundation of your relationship. To ensure that this soul connection lasts for many years, you must maintain it. Spend more time together, embrace, pay more attention to each other, give gifts, show care, support each other in difficult times, seek compromises in disputes, and much more. It's impossible to list everything in one paragraph; this is a topic for a separate book on relationship psychology. The main thing is to find what works best for you and your partner and use it daily! Continuously nurture and expand the connection between your inner energies – your Love!

Married life is not all happiness; it's daily self-improvement and working on your relationship as a couple. You won't be able to spend 100 years in marriage without arguing with your partner, clarifying your relationship, or listening to reproaches. You might even have a few arguments. At some point, thoughts of breaking up your relationship or getting a divorce may cross your mind. All of this is related to your soul's "negative" energy. It will often seek to nourish itself energetically from your negative emotions. You or your better half might not show your best side in these moments. To avoid this, you must recognize the problem, understand your partner's emotions, learn to smooth conflicts, and compromise. This way, you can live a long and happy life together, regardless of hardships.

As for me, I met my love 25 years ago. My future wife, Hanna, came to study at our high school in the 9th grade. She had transferred from another school. I still remember the moment when she entered the classroom for the first time with her friend. It wasn't love at first sight, but it was destiny. My friend jokingly said, "This girl is mine, and you'll get the other one," pointing to my future wife. Those words turned out to be prophetic.

Before becoming a "couple in love," Hanna and I became friends and built a strong friendship. We shared many common interests, enjoyed spending time together, and understood each other without many words. This friendship was built on the connection between "soulmates." As the saying goes, "Friends are either former or future lovers." That's what happened to us. We kissed for the first time as we watched the sunrise at our high school prom. After that, our love was born, and the connection between our souls grew stronger with each passing day.

We were in a relationship for four years. Now we have been married for eighteen years. It's not long, but I hope, as in our wedding vow, "We will live long and happy lives and die on the same day." Throughout our long life together, many events have tested the strength of our love. We've had our ups and downs. Sometimes, we argued and fought, but we always found common ground, discussed our problems, made peace, and moved forward.

I am happy in marriage. I love Hanna with all my heart and soul. And I thank the Universe for sending me my other half, my love for life. I am grateful to Hanna for always being there and supporting me. I'm thankful for our wonderful children, daughter Yeva and son Lev. For the happy moments we've shared! Thank you, my dear. I love you!

Creating a family taught me many things. I experienced many vivid emotions, the most intense being the births of our children.

* * *

The love between partners and parents' love for their children is different expressions. No matter how deeply you love your significant other, with the birth of a child, you experience an extra, deeper, and purer love.

This is because a newborn child, their biological shell, is a part of the mother and the father. Your DNA combines with your partner's DNA, giving birth to a new person with your shared genetic code. Your essence will always be a part of them, your blood. This connection binds you forever. And your child's soul is so new and pure that with the first contact and gaze into their eyes, you'll feel a unique bond, a new love forming between you.

The more time you spend with your child, the more you hug them, care for them, and express your love, and the stronger your connection with them! A child is happy when they have loving parents by their side. Meanwhile, the child's happy soul grows more vital, and their love for their parents grows daily.

I experienced this profound feeling of a parent's love for their child when I first saw my daughter, Yeva. At that moment, this little human became my entire Universe. I couldn't take my eyes off her. It so happened that the first few days after the difficult birth, our baby wasn't with us. But when they brought her to our room, and we could hold her, I felt a more incredible surge of love. I didn't want to let go of her, and I wanted to gaze at her for eternity.

My beloved daughter is growing and becoming wiser and more beautiful. Even though she's now a teenager with a formed personality and her worldview, I love her just as deeply. I will love her always! Our bond is unbreakable!

With the birth of my son, Lev, I experienced a new burst of energy—the same feeling of Universal Happiness I had when my daughter was born. I was present at both births. There were complications When Yeva was born, and I was asked to leave the delivery room even before dawn. But when my son was born, I could support my wife throughout this challenging process and be there until our son was born. At that moment, when he was first placed on my wife's belly, my love for my son was born. His little fingers gently embraced Hanna. His eyes were barely open, and his mouth searched for milk. The image of this little "bundle of happiness" will remain in my heart forever, just like my first meeting with my daughter. I love them both so profoundly!

I am infinitely grateful to my beloved wife, Hanna, my other half, for our children! They are the fruit of our love! And I thank the Universe for this incredible miracle—the birth of new life!

I know, I know. Most men are afraid to be present at childbirth. But it's not something to fear or avoid. I was there twice. I'm fine: my limbs are intact, my mind is sound, and I don't have nightmares. Being present at childbirth provides essential moral support to your loved one. Plus, the emotions of witnessing your child's birth will ignite a love within you of such strength that you can carry it through your entire life and beyond. That's why, generally, women tend to love their children more intensely than men. They understand the value of giving birth to a new person. They experience that emotional surge of Universal Happiness in the first moments of a child's life, having gone through the challenging process of childbirth. I recommend to all men to be present at the birth of their children!

Most of the time, the love between parents and children is mutual and nonconditional. However, sometimes exceptions occur when love doesn't develop. This can lead to a detachment of souls, and parents may be unable to love their children. This creates many difficulties within the family, misunderstandings, conflicts, and even hatred. It's like a parent living under the same roof as a stranger. Fortunately, this is rare. Therefore, attend childbirth together with your partner. Support your significant other and share this unforgettable and unique experience. It will strengthen your love for each other and the little one!

* * *

Love between brothers and sisters is another form of connection among human souls. This love differs from other expressions of love. Such kinship is more based on the awareness that you are part of the same cell or family. You share familiar parents, and your DNA contains a shared foundation. Your flesh and blood are the legacy of your parents. Your connection with brothers and sisters is fundamentally strong—you are kindred souls by birth!

Many will say their relationships with brothers and sisters are complex and sometimes even catastrophic. This is certainly possible. The reason for this lies in negative emotions that feed from within. For example, there is always something to share with siblings: toys, rooms, parental attention, friends, etc. This always leads to conflicts. If you don't learn how to cope with these emotions, they can lead to sad consequences.

The basis of relationships with brothers and sisters should be built on the understanding that you are one family. After all, when parents take their place on the Family Tree, no one will be closer and dearer on Earth than them. Some may say that their spouse is more beloved to them. But what if you fall out of love with them or part ways? What remains after that? You have something more significant with brothers and sisters than soulful love. You share the same blood and the fruits of the same tree. Let this thought help you overcome all disagreements with your loved ones. You are bound by the same strong family bond only with your children—through flesh, blood, and soul.

I know exactly what I'm talking about. I have an older brother and a younger sister. Like all children, we shared things in our childhood, settled our differences, and sometimes fought, but we always found the strength to measure ourselves and be one family. Even though our parents are no longer with us, and my brother and sister are thousands of kilometers away, they are still my family, and I love them just as deeply as before.

* * *

My love for my parents is as strong as my love for my children, beloved wife, brother, and sister. Our parents were a shining example of a strong family for many years. They instilled the foundation of family values in me. My parents taught me to love my loved ones and to care for them. They showed me how to build a happy family with the person I love. With her tenderness and love, Mom, Irina, demonstrated how to be a good parent. Dad, Valerii, with his wisdom, care, and sense of humor, taught me how to be a father, the head of a family, and a better person. I am deeply grateful to them for this!

To my great regret, over time, their decades-long relationship weakened, developed cracks, and eventually fell apart. But Mom and Dad remained my parents, my family, and my loved ones until their lives were cut short. They took their place on our Family Tree alongside our grandparents. As long as my brother, sister, our children, and I remember them, they will live forever and watch over us. I believe that "there" they found peace and happiness together again. After all, the strength of their soul connection was immense.

The love between souls is born in life, extends over many years, and does not cease even after the death of biological shells. By working on your relationships and nurturing the connection between your soul and your partner's soul, you weave them together stronger and stronger. Ultimately, you will never lose yourselves in the boundless expanses of Universal Energy.

The entire Universe is infused with Love! It can exist between partners, towards your children, between brothers and sisters, and even extend to your kindred souls and the Universe itself! The Family Channel is the door to the Universe, and Love for your kindred souls is the key. Love is the adhesive that holds the entire Universe together!

The next chapter will explore who these "kindred souls" are and why finding them is essential.

KINDRED SOULS

“

"The most significant particles of the Universe - your kindred souls."

”

At present, the Earth's population stands at around 8 billion people. This number may seem impressive. But let's put it into the context of the entire Universe. According to scientists' estimates, in our Milky Way galaxy alone, there are between 100 to 400 billion stars, and in the whole Universe, there are approximately 200 billion galaxies. It's mind-boggling! So, what does that say about us, you and me - specks in this vast Universe? An adult human body consists of approximately 30 trillion cells! Therefore, each one of us contains our Universe.

Once we realize the scale of the Universe and the biological world within us, the figure of 8 billion people no longer seems imposing. Nevertheless, it is not insignificant. Yet, people often feel lonely despite this. Why is that? Along our life's journey, we encounter only a few individuals who are kindred spirits. We form friendships, build relationships, create families, and grow old together with them.

How many people do we meet throughout our lives? From a thousand to a million? Should we count those we've merely met or with whom we've had a single conversation? Of all the people we've encountered, communicated with, or worked alongside, how many become truly close to us? A dozen or two? And who are those fortunate few with whom we feel a solid connection, pulling us toward them like a magnet? These are our "Kindred Souls."

Numerous people come into our lives, each with their mission: to teach us something new, help us through tough times, share our joys and sorrows, impart life lessons, or forever change our lives. All these people - acquaintances, friends, relatives, our significant others - but how can we discern those spiritually close to us, stand out from the crowd and become essential to us? The answer is the same: these are our kindred souls.

So, who are these kindred souls? They are particles of Universal Energy drawn to our souls more strongly than others. The force of attraction between them arises instantly and overgrows. You will immediately sense that they are "your people." Being with them will always feel comfortable, and you'll be "on the same wavelength," understanding each other with just a few words.

This connection may be vital because your souls have already interacted in past lives. Therefore, you've met again in this incarnation to embark on a new life journey together. Or the birth of a new connection will last centuries. The key thing to understand is that kindred souls are energetically linked to varying degrees. Yet, all your kindred souls are part of your energetic system, your life, your Universe, and a part of yourselves.

There are several groups of kindred souls, each with its unique physical and spiritual relationships. The first and foremost group is the "Family." These are your close relatives: grandparents, parents, siblings, your significant other, and your children. The second group we'll call "Friends," which includes numerous people. I want to highlight the "best friends" category as an intermediate link between family and friends.

With family, you share a strong, energetic connection from birth. They are your kindred souls with the strongest bond. This bond is founded on Love, the most powerful magnet for souls in the Universe. You don't choose your family; you are born into it. You become a part of it. Your significant other also becomes part of your family. They are the only members of your family whom you choose based on the call of the heart. Your family, your kin, forms the densest cluster of energetic particles around you in the Universe.

I have a large family. My beloved wife Hanna and our children Yeva and Lev are always by my side. I feel their love and energy every day. Universe, I thank you for this! Even though my brother and sister and their families are far away now, separated by thousands of kilometers, I always think of them and strive to stay in touch. I feel their warmth and spiritual closeness even on the other side of the world. Universe, thank you for my family! My grandparents and parents are no longer with us but always with me. I sense their presence and support every day. They are my Family Tree - the foundation of my connection to the Universe. They are the Universe to me!

In the category of "best friends," only a few people have entered my life over the years. My beloved wife is one of them. The energetic connection between us has grown to unparalleled proportions and serves as the foundation of our family.

Back in University, I had a friend named Dima. He was so spiritually and energetically close to me that I always felt we were "on the same wavelength." He was a true kindred soul to me. Unfortunately, time and distance gradually eroded our friendship and our spiritual connection. We didn't argue or part ways for specific reasons. It's just that our communication became less frequent, and our energetic connection began to fade and eventually evaporated. I sometimes think of my university friend. Those are good memories. I'm grateful to the Universe for that person and our wonderful time together.

How strong is the bond between kindred souls? How do they find each other? I'm sure that you will immediately sense comfort and warmth in the company of such a person, an invisible connection between you. It will feel like you've known each other for a hundred years.

That's how fate brought my best friend Alexander and me together. It's hard to believe, but we met him hundreds of kilometers away from home, in another country, during a vacation in Egypt. Upon returning home, we discovered that we had lived on the same street, just a few hundred meters apart, and had never crossed paths. Was it destined for us to meet? Most definitely. We bonded with our young families. My wife and I were married for two years while Alexander was on his honeymoon. We immediately found common ground, shared interests, and started spending a lot of time together. Then, our first children were born within a month of each other. Alexander became the godfather of my daughter. For many years now, we've been navigating life's challenges together. Even though an ocean separates us now, I always try to maintain contact with my best friend. I don't want to lose a spiritually close person again - my kindred soul.

We also have "excellent friends" with Hanna and me. They are also our kindred souls. They are part of our energy circle, part of our life. They are lovely and unique people! They are kind-hearted, talented, and humane in their unique ways. Each of them is dear to us and has become a good and faithful friend.

Some have grown a little closer, taking on the outstanding role of being the godparents of our son. However, we interact with all our friends equally and build friendships with their families. We strive to maintain friendly relationships despite distances and challenging times. We miss our large group of kindred souls dearly. Our side misses their warmth and energy. But we will surely meet again, embrace each other, recharge our energies from one another, smile, and step into a brighter future together. Thank you, Universe, for our friends!

I have also worked and studied with many people, some of whom have become close to me in spirit. We are scattered worldwide but stay connected and communicate thanks to modern technology. These people have taught me a lot, supported me, and had wonderful times with me. I am grateful to the Universe for allowing me to meet so many outstanding individuals on my life's journey!

My life has proven that we must cherish our kindred souls with all our might and always maintain a connection with them, no matter what. Neither time nor distance should be a barrier between you. Call, write, and meet with each other. Communicate more often. Show interest in their lives and share important events with them. Remember that they need you just as much as you need them! Cherish and value each other! It's easy to get lost and be alone in this world. It's much harder to find and keep your kindred souls. Remember, you and they are one whole energy node in the boundless Universe!

HOME

“

"Your Home is where your family is."

”

The notion of “Home” evokes different associations for each person. For some, it's the "four walls" in which they grew up. For others, it's their familiar and beloved city. And for some, it's their homeland, the country where they were born. I have experienced all these stages and found my "Home."

Our childhood and youth always pass in our parents' home. Hundreds of pleasant memories are associated with it. Your room and personal space, where you fought with your siblings. The smell of your mom's delicious meals in the kitchen and her lullabies at night. Your dad is sitting at the table, engrossed in constructing something fascinating. Your beloved pet is sleeping on your bed. Evening gatherings in front of the TV with the whole family. Loud celebrations and parties with friends and adults. First dates. For each of us, this place is filled with countless pleasant moments and memories that shape our concept of "Home." It's where you feel cozy, safe, and loved.

But can you consider your apartment or the house where you live as your “Home”? Is it truly yours? It seems that these "four walls" are undoubtedly an essential part of your life, but it's not your “Home”; it's a place of residence, no matter how dry that may sound. My parents and I lived in different apartments. There were three of them. Two were my grandmother's apartments, and one was my parents'. All three of these apartments were my "Home." Throughout my life, I've moved to approximately 14 different flats! And most of them were rented. My children are growing up primarily in rented housing. That's how fate has unfolded. In 2014, war came to our hometown of Donetsk in Ukraine, and we had to leave it, experiencing what it meant to live in a rented apartment.

If it's not housing that defines the concept of "Home," then what does? Perhaps the city where you were born and lived for many years since childhood? I loved my hometown of Donetsk very much. It was a beautiful "City of Roses" with just over one million people. We jokingly called it a "small village." Meeting a familiar face was not difficult; it was as if everyone knew each other, or at least a friend knew your friend. Over thirty years, Donetsk became a cozy and familiar home to me. Only pleasant memories remain quiet streets, beautiful parks, the central square, numerous residential areas where friends lived, schools and universities, cafes and nightclubs, the registry office where my family was "born," and thousands of other details.

Why did I say that Donetsk "was" my home? Because the war took it away from us. My wife, daughter, and I were forced to leave the city. We relocated to a safer place in the capital of Ukraine, Kyiv. This city became our new home. Kyiv is a massive metropolis with green streets, a beautiful historic center, numerous business districts, shopping centers, and residential areas. Over four million people pass by us daily, searching for a brighter future. Over time, the feeling of "Home" began to reemerge. We lived in many rented apartments and even took out a mortgage. However, it was not meant to be completed due to disputes between the authorities and businesses. This became one of the reasons, perhaps the final straw, in deciding to move again, but this time to another country.

A city cannot fully correspond to the concept of "Home" either. At this point, my family and I have lived in four different cities. Each became where I wanted to live and raise my children, but circumstances forced me to move on each time. It seems that a town, just like your "four walls," is not a "Home" in the broad sense of the word. It's your place of residence. So, what then defines the concept of "Home"? Maybe the country in which you live?

I was born in the USSR, a country that no longer exists. It dissolved in September 1991, forming several separate countries, including Ukraine. All that remains as a memory is my birth certificate with a green cover. An old, battered document, worn down by life and relocations and having no value or significance except as a piece of our history.

I was seven years old when the new state - independent Ukraine - was formed. Just yesterday, my brother was a Young Pioneer and was learning to tie a "Pioneer tie." And I, a first grader, was initiated into the "October Youth." Suddenly, in one moment, everything began to change. It came with new rules, values, a new language at school, a new currency, and many other changes.

In Ukraine, I lived for 30 years. Here, my childhood, youth, and adulthood passed by. I found my best friends here, built a family, and had children. Ukraine will always be associated with many pleasant and warm memories. It was my home and my homeland. I grew up here, my parents are buried here, and my siblings still live here. It was our home, but war and other circumstances forced us to seek a new, safer, and more reliable place.

So, Hanna, our children, and I found ourselves in Europe. In February 2021, we moved to Poland, the magical town on the Baltic Sea - Gdansk. This beautiful, charming, and cozy city became our new Home. My friend Andrei helped us with the move and adaptation. We met in Kyiv when we both started working on the same day at a new IT company. We immediately found common ground and shared interests, and our friendship was born. So, I gained one more kindred soul.

My family and I lived in Gdansk for just over a year. It was a wonderful time. We loved the cozy and beautiful city by the sea. Friendly and smiling Poles treated us well. My daughter made new friends and completed the seventh grade in a Polish-language school. We even started considering the possibility of staying there permanently.

But on February 24, 2022, Russia launched a full-scale invasion of Ukraine. A new, more horrifying stage of the war began. It continues to this day as I write these lines. Part of my country is under the occupier's control. My hometown is now part of another country. While Ukrainians fight for their land at the cost of their lives, my soul aches for them, and I pray to the Universe for peace and a swift victory.

The escalation of the war and increasing tension on the border with Poland made me think about the safety of living here. I returned to the idea of migrating to Canada. I started looking for a way to make this dream a reality. At that moment, Canada launched a new immigration program that opened the doors for us to move. I discussed this possibility with my family and employer, and with their approval, we flew to fulfill our long-held dream of living in Canada.

Will Canada become our home? Possibly. I hope so. But I can say that a country, in the sense I associate with the word "Home," doesn't fully capture it. So, if it's not housing, a city, or a country, what is our home? Maybe it's our "homeland"? Whatever that may mean to each of us. Or perhaps it's the land where we were born?

Ukraine will forever remain my homeland. But I have a broader concept of "Home." If you think of Home as your apartment, you only care about cleanliness and comfort within those walls. If you expand your Home boundaries to the entire building, you start watching about the entrance and the surrounding area. Go further, and it's your neighborhood, city, and country. The wider the boundaries of your "Home," the more significant things you begin to care for and protect. My Home's boundaries encompass the entire world! I'm an Earthling, a "Citizen of the World" or, if you prefer, a "Resident of the Universe." I am not alien to the lives of other people and living beings, the peace and tranquility in different corners of our planet.

You have a solid emotional, spiritual, and energetic attachment to the land where you were born and raised. But in the modern world, it's not uncommon to move from place to place, either out of necessity or by choice. This means you cannot spend your entire life in one place. And the land where you were born may not be your Home forever.

My friend used to joke, "Home is where your 'butt' is warm." There's some truth in that joke. At a certain point in life, I thought, "What if we remove the borders of countries? Where will I live then? What will be my 'homeland' or 'native land'?" The answer came naturally. I was born on planet Earth. I am an Earthling! This means that the whole planet will become my enormous "Home." And if they issue me a "passport of an Earthling," I will travel freely around the globe and live wherever I wish. I've been living with this thought ever since. I move from one apartment to another, from one city to another, from one country to another, and from one continent to another.

But even this didn't fully define the concept of "Home" for me. After analyzing all my wanderings, I realized what indeed constitutes my Home. What is that integral "element" of my life that is always with me, that I travel with, and that always provides a sense of home wherever I go and wherever I live? This secret ingredient of my feeling of Home is my Family!

"Your Home is where your Family is!"

This truth wasn't clear to me immediately, but it has made me happy! Regardless of the housing, city, or country, I may find myself in, I am so glad if my beloved and dear ones are with me! And I know that "I am Home!"

Your family is the energetic center of your Universe. This potent concentration of Universal Energy around you will always protect you and provide warmth, comfort, hope, and love. Wherever you live in this Universe, if your family is with you, know that "you are Home!"

HUMAN MEASURE

"The human mind - the connecting link between matter and energy in the Universe."

The human mind or the "Human Measure" is the key to everything in the Universe! In the description of the schema of the Universe, the brain plays a crucial role. It is the critical link in the interaction between humans and Universal Energy and matter. On one hand, the brain is the center for processing information gathered through various measures. On the other hand, it is the source of our internal energy, connecting it with Universal Energy. Our brain is the link through which the Universe can interact with matter, study it, and modify it.

The foundation for collecting information about matter for the brain lies in our five senses: sight (eyes), touch (skin), hearing (ears), taste (tongue), and smell (nose). These five senses continuously gather primary information from the surrounding world for further processing by the brain. Our consciousness collects all this information, filters and processes it based on various measures, focusing on what is most important to us, and makes conclusions.

Thanks to the numerous measures devised by humanity, we can process the information we receive from the surrounding matter. The Measure has become the key to self-awareness and understanding of the Universe.

Our eyes perceive colors and shapes, but the measures of color and form help us comprehend them. The stimulation of taste receptors on the tongue conveys the taste of food, but tasting measures determine what is sour, sweet, bitter, tasteless, and so on. Receptors of touch on the skin transmit information about stimuli, but it is through measures that the brain understands what is hot or cold, pleasant, slippery, wet, and so forth. The same applies to hearing and smell. By receiving information from matter, we understand what is loud or quiet, what smells good, and what stinks.

As you may have noticed, many measures define pairs of opposites: cold - hot, large - small, white - black, loud - quiet, bittersweet, and so on. Some measures represent more than two properties, but the essence remains the same - everything is understood through comparison! Our brain is designed so that we cannot comprehend what is hot without feeling cold or how far something is without knowing what is close. This mechanism helps form many different measures through which we gather information.

Humans use many "basic" measures to process information from their senses. More importantly, our intellect can build "higher" measures based on them. These higher measures help us better describe complex processes in the Universe and gain a deeper understanding of it.

Human speech and writing are key higher measures. We have given names to everything that surrounds us, all the matters we have come to understand. People have named, described, and devised rules for all measures. We pass the accumulated information to our descendants through speech and writing.

The transmission of information from generation to generation is a critical factor in the spread of knowledge. But along with this advantage, we encounter a drawback. Over the years of evolution, humanity has developed numerous languages and dialects. This means that the more languages there are, the more different measures exist. Measures from other languages describe the same information and matter. Words in one language may mean nothing or sometimes even represent different concepts for someone with various linguistic measures. This is where problems with information transmission, communication breakdown, and misunderstanding between people begin.

Think back to the "spoon" from the first chapter. Which specific measure of language, i.e., word, did you use to describe this matter? Spoon. And what words do people from other languages use to describe this type of matter? Often, these names are similar; words are harmonious, especially among languages belonging to the same language groups. But sometimes, you may need help understanding what your interlocutor is saying or what is written in a language unfamiliar to you. It can even happen that people speaking the same language and using the same measures do not understand each other. This happens due to different figurative measures, where you name the same thing with different words or imply different concepts and processes with the exact phrase.

Various languages complicate communication between people of different nations. A solution could be a "universal set of linguistic measures." In other words, it is one language spoken by all of humanity. However, this task seems unachievable and could take hundreds or thousands of years. It may not be worth abolishing all the world's languages, leaving only one. Our languages are the legacy of our cultures, values, traditions, and measures of understanding the Universe.

To improve communication for all of humanity, it would be worthwhile to establish some "international language" as a basis. It would become a universal means of conveying information between different nations and would describe other measures and all matter in the Universe as accurately as possible. Humanity only needs to decide which language will become familiar to all. The main thing is to be relatively easy to learn while providing the most precise description of all matter, information, and other measures.

This is a reasonably achievable task for each of us - to learn two languages. After all, many people already speak multiple languages.

For example, my daughter Yeva knows four languages. And this is not the limit. Therefore, it is within the ability of each individual to master and use this "universal international language"!

* * *

An important point worth discussing is the different stages of brain development. They are abstract and do not have clear boundaries, but I believe you can quickly identify and recognize them.

A child's mind is as pure as a blank slate. It has yet to form independently or acquire knowledge from others. A baby's brain is just beginning to develop and collect its first information about the surrounding world. Adults with more developed brains teach children basic measures, new concepts, and language as the highest measure.

As a child grows older, their brain develops better. Here, it is crucial how adults help develop their thinking. With various methods and means of education, children's brains develop differently. The genetically determined potential we discussed earlier also plays a significant role in this process. Differences in development sometimes become evident and noticeable to the naked eye. However, this should not be a reason for one group of children to feel superior to others. This difference depends on many factors influencing a child's development: genetics, ways of perceiving information, and processing speed. Instead of criticizing the weaker results of some children compared to others, it is better to make extra efforts and find more effective teaching methods for these children.

The stages of brain development change throughout our entire lives, from infancy, childhood, adolescence, to adulthood and old age. All these stages are distinct, and people easily understand this. However, there are not only these stages of brain development but also degrees of intellectual development, as described in the example with children above.

In adults, the degrees of intellectual development are distinct enough to be seen by the naked eye. This relates to how a person develops their brain and learns throughout life. The longer and more effectively they are educated, the higher their intelligence will be. You can quickly notice the difference between an uneducated person with no opportunity to learn and develop and the best minds of humanity, such as Albert Einstein, Nicolaus Copernicus, Nikola Tesla, Elon Musk, and others. This fundamental difference, even a chasm, is immediately visible. But what lies between these diametrically opposite extremes?

It's important to understand that the human brain develops in stages, at varying speeds and up to certain limits. Therefore, there are several degrees of intellectual development. It would be best if you went through many stages of academic growth to reach from the starting point to genius. But it's worth it.

In today's reality, you must constantly learn and develop your brain throughout your life! This is very important! The quality of your life, its richness in happy moments, the fullness of sensations, abundance, and your degree of freedom depend on it!

In the modern world, not only the physically most robust Homo sapiens survive, but also those who have developed their brains more than others. People with higher intelligence can lead and manipulate the masses, guiding them and exerting influence. A high degree of intellectual development is the key to your freedom from "intellectual slavery"!

From the perspective of interaction with the Universe, the better your brain is developed, the better and more productively you can communicate with it. You can collect and process information about matter more effectively, generate new ideas, and create and change the matter around you, thus advancing humanity. And you will help the Universe develop, understand itself, and evolve.

* * *

The key to a free and happy life is mindfulness at every moment. Living a mindful life means not letting it flow aimlessly and not going with the current.

Our brain is designed so that some processes occur in an unconscious mode. And that's great! I wouldn't want to think about every movement of my hand while scooping food with a spoon and putting it in my mouth. Let alone consciously control routine processes like walking, breathing, etc. But one of the properties of our brain is its ability to simplify, automate, and shift into unconscious control. It sometimes does this so well that a significant part of a person's life goes on in "unconscious mode," "going with the flow," "autopilot," or "fate has it so."

Conscious control of your thoughts, decisions, and actions is what you need to develop in yourself! Mindfulness will help you change your destiny, influence the course of events, and ultimately take control of it. You can only live a happy, long, and eventful life by "taking the helm into your own hands."

Learn to be aware of what you are doing at any given moment. It's akin to waking up in the morning. You control very little in your sleep, but you can change the course of events upon awakening. In moments of mindfulness, you wake up, look around, and understand what's happening and how you can influence it.

This handy skill will help you avoid many problems in your life and improve its quality. I strive to be mindful in various life situations: when making important decisions, when following a pre-established plan, when searching for life goals, and when interacting with people.

For example, when there's a conflict or tension in my family, and emotions are running high, I exercise self-control. I don't allow myself to be carried away by emotions and vent everything, I think. Recognizing the situation's complexity, I try to reduce tension, calm those close to me, and propose compromises. It's mindfulness that helps me avoid conflicts. Of course, I don't control all such situations, and sometimes emotions take over, but I'm learning, evolving, and trying to live a more mindful life.

There have been examples of unconscious decisions that influenced my entire future—for instance, the choice of my profession. My older brother studied "Computer Engineering" at university for two years. I occasionally witnessed significant challenges in his studies, which deterred me from choosing the same field. However, I loved computers, and everything related to them. I was deeply interested in the subject. My brother and I could spend hours, even days, studying the inner workings of computers, playing games on them, chatting in forums, and doing plenty of helpful work for school and university.

When choosing my future profession, I attended an open house event at the same university my brother attended. I was confident that I wanted to avoid following in his footsteps. When my father handed me a brochure listing various computer-related professions with complex and incomprehensible words like Delphi, Assembler, C++, Databases, Operational Systems, etc., I made a Fateful Unconscious choice.

I should have delved deeper into studying the professions' structures, opportunities, or prospects. Instead, I was drawn to a description filled with beautiful and incomprehensible words. I thought it sounded "cool." Without thinking much about the consequences of that decision, I pointed at a random profession in the brochure and said to my father, "I'll study here." This unconscious choice led me to become a "Software Developer for Automated Systems."

I realized how challenging this profession was during my first year at university. It was difficult for me to study. I became less enthusiastic about becoming a programmer. In the first higher mathematics class, the instructor said, "Congratulations! You've chosen the least promising profession! Managers, for example, can climb the career ladder to the very top. But all you'll be able to do is write code with no growth prospects."

However, over time, my brain filled with knowledge. I developed an interest in learning, and subjects became easier to grasp. Still, I didn't want to connect my future life with this profession. The motivation to finish my degree came from my father's advice: "You must have a higher education to secure a good job and provide for yourself and your family."

I graduated from university and took a job, but not in my field of study. I went wherever I could find employment. I started as a salesperson in a store selling household and computer equipment. Two years later, I entered the banking industry as an administrator for payment systems. I didn't work in my chosen profession for the next eight years. When I made that choice at university, I had no idea how much the world would change and how in-demand the work of a programmer would become ten years later. Fortunately, the Universe guided me in the right direction while I was on autopilot.

In 2014, when the war broke out in our hometown, my family and I were forced to move to a safe place. We relocated to the capital of Ukraine, Kyiv, and started a new life from scratch.

Life in Kyiv was costly, even for me, who moved with a job in the bank. All I had at that time was my wife, our little daughter, and a couple of bags of clothes. My salary barely covered the cost of renting a small one-bedroom apartment and a meagre supply of groceries. During this challenging period, I learned to become mindful and take control of my destiny. I started thinking about improving our situation and providing my family with a better life.

In a state of awareness, I began to analyze my skills and explore job opportunities in the labor market to find a higher-paying job. "What am I good at? What skills do I possess? What do I want to do?" I pondered various questions. At some point, I remembered my education and the fact that I am a creative person.

Throughout my life, I have been creating things. I wrote poetry and songs, scripts for movies, and described ideas for computer games. Now, I'm writing a book. My creative energy always sought an outlet. However, I had yet to learn how to make a living from it and support my family. The idea of pursuing a creative profession was quickly dismissed because I needed a solution here and now before the situation became catastrophic.

I found information online about the modern realities of the job market for programmers in Kyiv and the earnings in this field. I was pleasantly surprised. The profession of programmer was in high demand and offered better pay than my job at the bank. I realized that my math teacher was wrong about the prospects of this specialty. And I had made a big mistake by not becoming a programmer ten years ago. Plus, the idea of writing code was very appealing. After all, it was also a form of creative work. I could create something "with my own hands" again! So, I finally decided to become a programmer.

I arrived at this decision consciously. But it was more complicated. I hadn't been developing in this direction and hadn't worked in the field for over ten years! I had forgotten everything. The only things I had left from five years of university education were my diploma and fond memories of my student years and friends. As I soon discovered, not all was lost, and I was able to recover some of the knowledge quickly.

Having made the conscious decision to become a programmer, I started learning a new programming language, Java, which was unfamiliar to me. I spent almost a year learning independently and taking various courses in the evenings, on weekends, and on holidays. Only after that did I find my first job in the field. It was a Junior Java Developer position, and my journey as a programmer was beginning.

Making the tough decision to start a new career was again guided by mindfulness. I was offered to create a new profession from the bottom. Meanwhile, I had succeeded at the bank, and a promotion to department head was on the horizon. What tipped the scales in favor of programming was that the salary for the Junior Developer position was almost the same as for the bank department head. I was offered to leave my "comfortable seat" in a stable bank and exchange it for unfamiliar work with an unknown client in an "office" in a rented apartment in Kyiv. And the job offer was made to me in a cafe, not at the company's main office.

It was challenging to exchange stability for uncertainty. But the prospects were much more important than a comfortable position. So, I made my choice and became a programmer! I'm grateful to the Universe for that choice! A conscious choice! It helped me change my entire subsequent life! I changed several employers and countries. Ultimately, I could move to the land of my dreams - Canada. I increased my income several times, allowing my whole family to live comfortably.

This was my conscious decision - to retrain as a programmer. I am very grateful to the Universe for not abandoning me during my unconscious career choice and guiding me on the right path! My university diploma and unconscious choice opened the doors to a future move abroad and a new, happy life.

And to think about how many people make the most critical decisions in their lives unconsciously. They choose their future profession, employers, and life partners, buy the "wrong" house in the "wrong" place, make the "wrong" decisions, and so on.

Only your mindfulness in thoughts, situations, actions, and decisions will help you live the life you want and deserve! Don't let other people and circumstances decide for you and make your life unconscious. Live consciously every day! If necessary, swim against the current and change your destiny! This life is yours, and only you can and should control it!

INTERACTION WITH THE UNIVERSE

> *"The quality of your life depends on how you interact with the Universe."*

Interacting with the Universe is a complex process. Still, if you take a closer look, follow simple rules, and fill yourself with energy, you can live a long, happy life full of unforgettable moments with your kindred souls.

In this chapter, I would like to share my vision of how everything around us is structured and interacts, and most importantly, how to become a part of this magnificence called Life.

We have become acquainted with the basic concepts of the Creation of the Universe, such as Matter - Information - Measure. We have discussed the structure of the Universe, in which your biological shell, your inner particle of Universal Energy, matter, and the energy of the Universe itself coexist harmoniously. You have learned how the Family Channel connects your soul and the Universe and how Love for the souls of your ancestors in the Family Tree helps strengthen this connection. You have realized your brain and consciousness's important role in this.

Now, all that remains is to clarify how these elements interact with each other and for what purpose. Open your mind wider! Absorb new information and explore new measures. They will help you answer the two most important questions people have been asking themselves for millennia: "Who am I? And why am I here?"

THE CONDUCTOR OF LIFE

What is Life? Life is the infusion of Universal Energy into the matter. The Universe lives, studies itself, learns from its experiments, evolves, changes, and perfects itself. This is the endless process of Life in the Universe. It must be cherished and valued as a gift, not taken for granted.

The Universe is a unified organism with numerous forms of life within it. In us humans, there exists a whole universe of cells, bacteria, and microorganisms. Similarly, the Universe has plants, insects, animals, birds, and humans. Both on Earth and possibly in other corners of the Universe.

The interaction of Universal Energy with matter occurs through all these living beings. The Universe studies, changes, and improves matter through them. Humans are the highest measure through which the Universe learns and changes itself.

Evolution is the development of matter by Universal Energy. For millennia, the Universe created new forms of life from various matter. These forms adapt, mutate, and die when no longer needed. The key is that the process of evolution never stops for a moment. Extinct species make way for the existence of others. History is replete with such cases, not to mention the dinosaurs!

Humans are not exempt from this evolutionary path of the Universe. Our biological shell is mortal and must be perfected in evolution. Immortality would halt the process of perfecting Life in the Universe. Whether the human species survives and how it evolves depends mainly on us. At the moment, we are at the pinnacle of evolution. But how successful an experiment are we for the Universe? How perfect are we? Time and the Universe will provide answers to these questions.

My father had a fantastic sense of humor, was witty, and knew hundreds of jokes for any occasion. Through these jokes and anecdotes, he passed on life wisdom to us, his children. One such story was about the duration of human life.

"Albert Einstein, after his death, found himself in heaven. There, he met God.

- Albert, I will give you the answer to any question. What would you like to know?" God asked.
- "Please, write down the formula for Human Life," Einstein replied.

- God nodded. A considerable board appeared in the sky with a complex and very long formula for Life.
- Einstein silently approached the board and started studying the formula. After some time, he turned to God.
- God, your formula for Life is magnificent! But... there's an error in the fourth line!
- I know," God replied, "...that's why you're here!"

If we abstract from various forms of life, such as humans, animals, and so on, and imagine that billions of particles of Universal Energy, souls of those very forms of life, live on Earth, the question arises: how do these particles interact with the General Universal Energy during their existence?

Here comes the idea of "conducting" the Universe with all this "orchestra of souls." The Universe interacts with absolutely every soul but to varying degrees. It depends on your faith, knowledge, and the emotional intensity of your thoughts.

The Universe hears each one of us without exception. It responds to our thoughts, words, and prayers through which we send our requests and desires. Each of us has specific needs and wishes. At any given moment, by thinking about them, we send energetic waves into the Universe. It accepts them as they are, without filters or limitations. Everything you think about, whether good or bad, reaches the Universe.

The Universe hears and responds to each of us, regardless of our requests. The response always comes but at different times. The time it takes for wishes to be fulfilled depends on many factors. Primarily, it's the energy behind your message to the Universe. The strength with which you desire something. The second factor is the overall energetic flow of desires and the possibility of their simultaneous fulfillment.

Imagine eight billion people who are constantly asking the Universe for something. How do you manage such a flow of desires? Is it possible to fulfill everything at once? What would happen if everyone on Earth wished for an elephant? The answer is simple. Not all wishes can be fulfilled at once! And thank the Universe for working this way! Otherwise, what would we do with eight billion elephants?

But what will happen if everyone continues to dream about elephants? Some people will quickly become disappointed that the elephant didn't appear "here and now" and will stop wanting it. Others will hold on to a bit longer. They'll dream for a day, a week, a month, but it will remain a weak desire with a low energetic signal sent into the Universe. The third group will turn to their faith, approach their idol, and pray, sending stronger signals to the Universe. Some will go even further. They'll create a mental image or a picture. They'll aim to " acquire a specific small gray elephant next year." They'll devise a plan to achieve this and start acting.

The Universe will respond to all these energetic signals differently. It's as if you have fifteen children who want something simultaneously. They all pester you, tug at you, and ask for something different. But some do it reluctantly, others ask too quietly, and the third group constantly pulls at your clothes and shouts, "I want! I want! I want!" You love all your children equally. But let's be honest, to whom will you give what they ask for first? The strength of desire plays an important role, but it's not the only factor.

The third essential component of getting what you desire is the Universe's ability to give it to you. Your children might all want chocolate candy at the same time. But if you only have one, you can satisfy the desire of only one child. And that's normal. In the Universe, there's enough for everyone. But sometimes, you must make extra efforts to get what you desire. For example, you might need to go to the store and buy more candy so that there's enough for all the children.

The fourth factor is time. It takes different amounts of time to obtain what you desire. For instance, it takes half an hour to drive to the store, several hours to walk there, or maybe a few days to make candies from scratch.

Let's return to the example of elephants for eight billion people. Those who don't give up will get elephants. Those who wished the hardest and followed a plan to achieve their goal. However, they will receive elephants at different times. It depends on the number of elephants on Earth. How many elephants are there in total? How quickly do they reproduce? Is it possible to clone them? There's an apparent quantitative increase in the elephant population at any given moment, and it will gradually satisfy the needs of those who request them.

In addition, the Universe will distribute existing elephants depending on a person's location, timing, and circumstances. For example, you might visit a zoo where a baby elephant was born today by luck. The zoo director has no available enclosures or funds to care for it further. By chance, you have an extra million dollars. That means you have every opportunity to buy it here and now! Congratulations! You've become the happy owner of an elephant! You can't say the same for someone in a remote northern area who has never seen an elephant and cannot buy one.

But take a moment to think about this beautiful chain of events that allowed you to buy an elephant. Is it luck or fate? How many occasions had to occur before you found yourself in the right place, at the right time, with the right opportunities? When did this zoo open? How long have they been keeping elephants there? Do you live in this city? Or did you come on vacation? Maybe you were visiting a friend? How did it happen that the elephant gave birth today? And what series of life events allowed you to become wealthy enough to have the required amount of money at that moment? And so on.

If you try to analyze this chain of events, you'll inevitably start to believe in fate, luck, gifts from the heavens, and other manifestations of higher powers. How does the Universe manage to organize all this? It's the conductor of the orchestra called Life!

When a new desire emerges, a new energetic flow, the Universe strives to incorporate it into the overall symphony of events to fulfill your wishes. This is undoubtedly a complex process. You need to pull dozens of strings, create numerous events, establish long cause-and-effect relationships, and add your desire so that it doesn't contradict others and disrupt the existing order of things. The task looks pretty complex, but that's why the Universe is there, as a "higher power" to solve it.

Perhaps this orchestra won't play perfectly, but it's essential to understand that you will get what you want "with all your heart" and "with all your soul" ! It could be under different circumstances, at an additional time, or in another form, but you will definitely receive it! Like a genie from a lamp, the Universe will respond to any request with, "As you wish!" and will fulfill it. Believe in the Universe, in your thoughts and desires, make plans and set goals, act, and wait without losing hope! And gather much patience because the Universe needs to find a way to provide eight billion elephants!

Listening to the Universe is crucial on the path to realizing your dreams. To correctly construct a chain of events from the multitude of possibilities, manifest them, and achieve your desires, the Universe will send you and the people around you hints and guide you in various ways. Why is this necessary? As you may recall, our soul originates and develops within our biological shell. The sole energetic connection of the soul with the Universe occurs through your brain and the Family Channel. The most important thing is that our soul is autonomous and not controlled by the Universe! We have the right to manage our lives and time as we see fit. This means that the Universe cannot directly manipulate us like puppets or chess pieces.

Humans always have a choice! The Universe can provide hints, guides, and point the way but cannot completely control us. Otherwise, we would be mere unconscious dolls. The Universe will communicate with you through hints and signs to redirect the energy flow in the right direction, alter matter, events, etc.

These signs and hints can vary. You might accidentally come across an advertisement for the sale of an elephant in a newspaper left at your neighbor's doorstep. Or an old friend might tell you about an exciting video where someone has already purchased an elephant and shares their experience on how to do it. Perhaps a random seatmate on an airplane sitting next to you turns out to be a zoo director. Anything can happen at any time, from small and barely noticeable nudges to clearly visible signs. What matters is how well you can listen to the Universe and recognize its hints.

The critical thing to remember is that "by missing a few gentle pushes in the back, you might receive a strong kick in the rear!" The Universe will still strive to fulfill everything that's been planned. If you listen and respond to the hints, the situation may work out in your favor, and you'll achieve the desired result.

Conducting Life, Energy, and Matter is an incredibly complex and all-encompassing! Through it, the Universe fulfills our desires and embodies its evolutionary needs, allowing life to develop, change, and thrive. Our unique lives represent new knowledge and experiences for the Universe.

I want to give you a couple more ideas for contemplation.

What is the human mind and our consciousness? It's ordered nerve impulses of energy between neurons in the brain. Millions of impulses per second are transmitted between nerve cells in different areas of the brain's hemispheres. The operation of our brain is a massive exchange of energy between neurons. All this energy is organized into more complex constructs: thoughts, words, images, ideas, dreams, and reactions to stimuli from our sensory organs. Eventually, all this energy forms the thinking process in our minds, giving rise to our consciousness, capable of governing our lives.

The Universe is a living organism. It contains an uncountable amount of matter and Universal Energy. This energy circulates between living beings and in a form free from matter in the General Universal Energy field. The Universe, through this energy, controls all processes and life. Energy moves between the "neurons of the Universe," forming processes like our brains, where consciousness exists. This raises an obvious question. Does the Universe have consciousness? Do the streams of Universal Energy create something akin to our consciousness? Or perhaps this is the "God" we cannot yet comprehend? I'll leave you alone with these thoughts, and for now, let's continue exploring the Universe and our role in the orchestra called "Life."

HAPPINESS

As we've discussed, a fragment of Universal Energy resides in each of us. It's our Soul. The amount of energy in each person's soul is different. If you've lived a life filled with more negative emotions than positive ones, your soul won't be significantly enriched energetically. And the size of your soul will be small, meagre. The opposite effect can be achieved by living a life full of positive emotions. They will make you happy and help your soul recharge energetically to the point where it begins to "shine." It's no coincidence that people say a person "shines" with happiness.

Happiness is the most powerful emotion of a human being! It arises in those moments when we experience strong positive emotions, thereby feeding the soul's energy. It only happens in specific moments, no longer. People often mistakenly believe happiness is a prolonged or constant state of being. This is not the case.

"I am happy" more accurately describes a specific moment when you are with a loved one: when your child is born, when you complete your education in school or university, when you're playing your favorite game, when you're sitting by the shore, savoring the sound of the ocean, when a dog licks your face in greeting. When a cat purrs and rubs against your leg, and so on. This list could go on indefinitely. Each of us experiences many such moments in life. They alternate with neutral or adverse events. But what matters is how many of these moments you have in your life and how happy a life you will lead!

We experience happiness and, in doing so, energetically charge ourselves through interactions with various forms of matter: water, fire, nature, art, family, friends, beloved hobbies, and so on. Through us, the Universe collects unique experiences from contact with various types of matter while simultaneously increasing its energy.

Each person is given a unique opportunity to live as their soul desires! The Universe may send us various hints and suggestions, but it has given us complete freedom to gain unique experiences.

Find the matter that makes you experience moments of the highest happiness and interact with it as often and for as long as possible! This determines the state of your soul, its energetic fullness, your psycho-emotional state, the purity of your thoughts, and, as a result, the quality of your life!

Do you enjoy petting your cat? Do you receive positive emotions from it, and does it make you happy? Then do it every day and as often as possible. You will experience happiness, and so will your cat. After all, a fragment of Universal Energy resides in them, too. Your regular touches will fill both of your souls with positive energy.

Do you enjoy collecting mushrooms? Running barefoot on sand or grass with morning dew? Just do it! Do you love hugging your loved one? Be together as often as possible. Do you love playing games with friends? Play! Do you like making model ships or collecting postage stamps? Can you compose poems, play a musical instrument, or paint pictures? You are lucky! Do everything that brings you joy! Remember, only you know how to make yourself happy! So, go ahead and do it! Live your unique life full of happiness, harmony, and love!

Another "balm for the soul" is interacting with nature and its elements. The world around us is infused with energy, which it will share with you if you desire. I'm sure you've noticed how water, especially in the sea and oceans, can calm a person, provide a sense of tranquility and happiness, and energetically recharge them. If you love water, go to the beach, dip your feet in the sea. Close your eyes and listen to the sound of the waves crashing against your feet. Feel that energy. Savor the moment of happiness. Water and other forms of natural matter, such as fire, earth, and wind, generate energy. Interact more with nature, charge yourself with its positive energy, and be happy!

My element is fire! It has beckoned me since childhood. There's something mystical about an open flame. Its energy recharges me and makes me happier. Whenever I can, I marvel at the dance of the fire. My eyes shine with happiness, and my soul "burns" after this kind of meditation.

Another "elixir for the soul" is music. It is rightfully one of the best inventions of humanity. It penetrates us so profoundly that it feels as if our soul is dancing to the melody of a beloved performer. I consider myself a music lover. I have the rudiments of musical hearing, although I lack a singing voice. I derive genuine pleasure from a good melody that caresses the ears. I've found happiness in listening to music of various genres and artists in different periods of life. But they have always been "melodies for the soul." If music makes you happy, listen to it more often! Sing, dance, enjoy, and be satisfied!

Even greater happiness comes from interacting and spending time with their kindred souls. Being in the family circle, playing with children, hugging loved ones, and engaging with dear friends can make you happier. These moments can give you unforgettable emotions and enrich your soul. So, spend time with your close and loved ones as often as possible! Put your phone and social media aside and embrace your loved one who's right there. Turn off that boring TV show and have a conversation with your children; play with them. Don't linger at the job you despise; instead, head Home, where you're awaited, loved, and can find happiness. Meet up with friends on the weekends. Spend an unforgettable evening together. Recall the good times with those who are no longer with you. They, too, want to be a little happier "there." Communicate, smile, and laugh with your kindred souls, and be satisfied!

What is a smile? Why do we laugh? Why do our eyes "shine" at certain moments? When does the soul smile? Where do tears come from when the moment is joyous? All of these are signs and indicators of happiness. Happiness is a powerful energy surge and an emotional uplift that our body expresses through a smile, laughter, and tears of joy. And there should be as many of these moments as possible! Let your soul begin to shine with joy! Live a happy and unique life! Become an integral part of Universal Energy! Be happy!

COMMUNICATION

Communication between the Universe and the Soul occurs through the medium of strong emotions and thoughts via our brain. Powerful emotional surges, such as despair, love, sincere desire, or intense concentration of thoughts, connect our soul to the Universe through the Family Tree or any other energetic channel. In this chain, the brain acts as an energetic center for receiving and transmitting thoughts to the Universe and back. The Family Channel amplifies their energy.

The path of thought movement in the Universe is as follows: our soul – the brain – the energetic channel (for example, the Family Tree) – the Universe. When the Universe responds to us, energy travels this path in reverse. This is the "technical side" of the communication process. But what is the purpose of this process? How can it be used productively?

Connecting to the Universe through the Family Channel gives our soul and brain a powerful, energetic charge. At this moment, the brain starts functioning much more productively than usual. The energy inside the brain becomes more robust, giving birth to new thoughts at a geometric rate. Neurons in your brain begin actively generating impulses and transmitting information. The stronger the connection between your soul and the Universe at this specific moment, the more effectively your brain will work. It will generate numerous thoughts and ideas and find the necessary answers to your questions.

The correct queries trigger the process of seeking answers in your brain. Great minds of humanity have said that "formulating the right question is difficult, but the answer will definitely be found." There is a practice like this: you ask yourself a question at night, and your brain subconsciously finds the answer during the night, which will spontaneously come to you in the morning. But now, I'm talking about the much greater potential of the brain than just finding an answer to some simple life question.

By using the Universe's energy during communication, incredible horizons for contemplation will open to you! You can generate ideas and find solutions to the most complex problems. You need a "strong and stable connection" with the Universe and your "right question."

There is a belief that in the Universe, there is a standard "repository of all knowledge" that, when connected to, a person can find an answer to any question or a solution to a complex problem. It's as if all knowledge about the Universe is stored in a vast library. You must reach out, take the right book, and find the answer. Many have mentioned this concept. For example, when Nikola Tesla was asked, "Where do you get ideas for your new devices?" he replied, "I don't know. They seem to come to me on their own from nowhere."

This appears to be like magic. You receive answers to all your questions without exerting special efforts or generating super-ideas.

It sounds enticing. But why are there so few brilliant inventions, works of art, or books containing all this knowledge? Why did the law of universal gravitation "fall" on Newton? Why could only Einstein describe the theory of relativity? And how did Mendeleev get lucky to see the periodic table of chemical elements in a dream? Where did Leonardo da Vinci's inventions come from? Perhaps all these great minds of humanity had their secret key to this "Universal Library of Knowledge"? And why don't you have it?

It's a little different. Indeed, all the necessary information is stored in the Universe. Think about matter, information, and measure. Absolutely ALL information describing it is contained within the matter itself. This means the entire Universe includes 100% of all the necessary information about itself. And all we need to do is select the proper measures to read this information. This means that the key to the "Universal Library" is our measures.

It works like this: by developing measures within us and gathering as much information about the matter around us as possible, we form a "copy of part of the knowledge from the Universal Library" in our minds. When you start the communication process with the Universe, you receive a tremendous influx of energy. The brain starts working in an "enhanced mode." By asking the "right questions," praying, or thinking about something, you search for answers and find solutions. In these moments, the brain can retrieve the necessary information from the deepest corners of your memory. It seems incredible that it remembers all of this. After acquiring all the required knowledge, the brain starts generating new ideas and finding answers to the questions posed.

Ideas and solutions don't come from nowhere. They are not sent to you by the Gods from the heavens. Ideas are born in your head. They are formed based on the information you already have! From your "copy of part of the knowledge from the Universal Library." This means that the more you develop your measures, acquire knowledge, and gather information about the surrounding world, the more of a foundation you will have for new ideas, insights, and discoveries.

The moments when you find answers, generate new ideas, and shout "Eureka!" can be figuratively labelled as "enlightenment" or "revelation." Enlightenment is also called a "meeting with the Muses." It is a "normal" creative process. Revelation is a deeper creative state of the mind. We will talk more about enlightenment and revelations in a separate chapter. It's important to understand that in these moments, your brain generates ("filters with a funnel") answers to questions, finds solutions, and so on.

What does "filters with a funnel" mean? Imagine an inverted funnel through which water is typically poured into narrow-neck bottles. At its base lies all the knowledge you've accumulated throughout your life. As the horn spirals upward, it narrows. With each new turn, relevant pieces of information connect while unnecessary ones are sifted out. Rising higher and higher, there's less knowledge, but its significance grows. Consequently, at the very top of the funnel, you obtain that knowledge or idea and seek that "Eureka !" moment and the answer to your question. The larger your foundation of knowledge and the base of your funnel in your mind, the greater the likelihood of finding the correct solution or generating an outstanding idea.

The knowledge thus filtered and acquired is passed from one person to another, forming new measures. The Universe gains experience and expertise through this filtration process, using them to transform matter. This is how thinkers, creators, and inventors influence the course of human history. For instance, Newton discovered the law of universal gravitation; the necessary knowledge was already in his mind. All he needed was the right moment of revelation.

One of the signs of such a "divine revelation" might be tingles on the skin, a surge of emotions, and so forth. You'll undoubtedly recognize these moments. To experience them more often, accumulate diverse knowledge, connect with the Universe, and generate new ideas. And remember to savor the results you obtain.

* * *

But how can you enhance the productivity of such communication processes and increase the quantity and quality of moments of revelation and enlightenment? There are specific "rituals" that can help you with this. Always strive to find the most effective options for yourself.

The formula for success is simple: "the right and quiet place – a comfortable posture – closed eyes – breathing – a clear mind."

The "right" place can be considered a location where you can be alone. It could be your room or office, a temple or church, a secluded spot in a park on a bench – any place where you can be alone with yourself and where there are as few "external distractions" as possible. Your senses should stop processing external information and sending it to your brain.

People who have brought new knowledge to humanity often distanced themselves from civilization in search of revelations and insights. They lived in solitude, entered temples, took sacred vows, and secluded themselves in forests or laboratories. Some even climbed mountains to receive their "Ten Commandments" from "God." It's as if genius is the domain of solitary thinkers.

With a "comfortable posture," things are more straightforward. Your body should be relaxed, and external distractions should be minimized. The calmer your nervous system, the less your brain will be distracted. Imagine composing a new "Moonlight Sonata" or inventing an anti-aging remedy when your stomach is constantly growling, your back aches, your nose itches, and your hand is swollen. The posture should be still, relaxed, and comfortable for you, such as lying in bed or sitting in a comfortable chair.

Keeping your eyes closed is advisable because most information reaches our brains through sight. Therefore, if you want to "go within," it's a good idea to close your eyes. Ideally, the surroundings should be dark, with minimal light seeping through your eyelids. I would also recommend focusing your gaze on the point between your eyebrows, often called the "third eye." This will help your eyes from darting around and concentrating on one thing. Don't worry; there will be something to see there. Your brain will conjure intricate shapes, patterns, and "swarms of ants scattering in different directions."

Breathing is no less critical in this system. Even calm and deep breathing will allow you to dive into your thoughts faster, improve oxygen flow to your brain, and keep you from getting distracted by the act of breathing. The teachings of yogis about breathing did not arise without reason. Proper breathing is crucial for achieving "nirvana."

The formula's most crucial element is a "clear mind." A calm, unclouded mind is much more productive. However, achieving this takes time and effort. It would be best not to think about anything other than the question. This is challenging and comes with practice. All the auxiliary elements mentioned above – the place, posture, closed eyes, and breathing – will help calm your mind. Otherwise, it's challenging to concentrate on the "idea that will make the world better" when you're thinking about food on the stove, children in diapers, a snoring spouse nearby, unfinished work, and so on.

By following the "formula for success," you will undoubtedly be able to communicate productively with the Universe, and you will indeed receive enlightenment, answers, or come up with new ideas.

I usually "connect" with the Universe by lying in bed at night in complete silence. As they say, you need to "sleep with the Muse" for her to bestow a new idea upon you. A soft bed, a relaxed posture, silence, and darkness, with no unnecessary thoughts – all help me concentrate on communicating with the Universe. How do you prevent yourself from falling asleep? That's a matter of practice and the strength of your desire to obtain Universal wisdom.

Closing my eyes, I visualize my Family Channel. I see the outlines of my mother and father's faces. I imagine hugging them tightly. I tell them how much I love them and miss them. The same goes for my two grandmothers and great-grandmothers. They are my family, my lineage, my Family Tree. Then, I express gratitude to them and the Universe for everything I have and hold dear for my beloved wife and children, my siblings, my sister and their families, and my extensive family scattered across different countries and continents. I express gratitude for friends, a roof over my head, a good job, food on the table, a safe place to live, good health, and life in general.

This is how I connect with the Universe through the Family Channel and initiate the communication process. There are several reasons why I do this. I pray to my ancestors and the Universe for the protection of my loved ones during these challenging times as the war rages in Ukraine. I seek assistance in my endeavors and the resolution of complex situations. Or I wait for the Muse to visit me while contemplating another idea.

I use communication with the Universe to search for new ideas and "communicate" with it. Otherwise, how would it know what I want? And how would I understand what it wants from me? But let's discuss everything step by step. First, let's learn to be grateful.

GRATITUDE

Gratitude is one of the most potent signals we can send to the Universe as "feedback." While interacting with people and matter, the Universe must somehow understand that its actions are correct and what results from its guidance, answers, and gifts. Gratitude is the best way to convey this.

Sincere gratitude "from the heart" or "from the soul" is a compelling emotion that generates a solid energetic signal to the Universe. The key here is your sincerity. It must be absolute and boundless. Sincerity plus gratitude equals a compelling, energetic message. It's like a direct connection of the soul to the Universe. This is why religions, and wise teachings place great importance on Gratitude to "their Gods" for what you already have and cherish.

Gratitude teaches you to value what you already have, something essential and allows you to cherish it even more. Be thankful for your family and loved ones as often as you can! So many people have lost their loved ones. And only after losing them do they begin to "value what they've lost." Don't wait until it's "too late." Love your family and loved ones here and now. Thank the Universe daily for their being alive, healthy, and safe! Many of us don't realize how important this is until tragedy strikes our doorstep. The war in Ukraine taught me to love my family and friends even more. The fear of losing them haunts me every day. And I ask the Universe, my Family Tree, to protect my loved ones and help them through these difficult times.

Thank the Universe for your life! For waking up this morning. For a new day and the opportunity to live it. Thank it for your biological shell, the health it brims with, and being whole and unharmed. And even if your body is not in "ideal condition" and you have "certain physiological limitations," be thankful for it because you are alive!

Thank the Universe for every moment spent with your family. The grief of losing loved ones is one of the worst feelings in the world! I know this is not just from hearsay. I first learned about death when my great-grandmother, Muma, passed away. I was too young to understand what had happened, but I knew she would never return.

Many years later, in my presence, cancer claimed the life of my beloved grandmother, Tasi (Anastasia). She was my father's mother. It was a profound shock for him. I had never seen such grief and horror on his face before. After her death, my father fell into a long-lasting depression. Sometimes, he would cry at her photos. He tried not to do it in front of us, his children, but emotions got the better of him. It hurt him. I saw his soul suffering. He even turned to religion for answers. He hung icons in our home and prayed to

God. And he kept asking the same questions repeatedly: "Why did my mother leave so soon? Why her? Why do good people go first?" These questions lingered in my memory for a long time. And so did my father's pain.

My mother's mother, Grandma Sveta, departed to the "other world." She passed away at 74 because of age and illness. She was fearless and one of those brave medics who helped contain the aftermath of the Chornobyl Nuclear Power Plant explosion 1986. While saving other people's lives, she received a dose of radiation sufficient to feel its effects for the rest of her life. Grandma Sveta was a strong person. Like Grandma Tasi, she raised her children on her own. I never knew my grandfathers. When I was born, they were no longer in our family. When Grandma Sveta passed away, my mother entered that same period of grief and despair my father experienced after Grandma Tasi's death. The pain of loss in my parents' eyes helped me understand how difficult it is to lose loved ones.

2020 was the most dreadful year of my life. It took away my mother and father. They passed away six months apart. My mother, Irina, was the first to go. Her death was sudden and swift. Her heart stopped. She was gone in a matter of minutes. I woke up to a phone call. It was my brother, Sergey, calling. My heart sank, and I felt an odd sense of dread. I picked up the phone and heard those ominous words: "Mom passed away..."

That dreadful feeling of losing a beloved person engulfed me like a tsunami from which there is no escape. It felt like a heavy weight crushing my chest. I couldn't breathe. Pain pierced me to my core. I cried. At that moment, I understood what my mother and father had felt when they lost their mothers. I experienced all the horror and pain they once did. Mom Irina was still so young, only 59 years old.

Dad Valerii joined the "other world" in the same year, six months after Mom's passing. He fell ill with what seemed like a common cold. But his condition deteriorated rapidly. Dad developed a severe cough, was plagued by fever and weakness, and his strength ebbed away. You could tell he was getting worse daily by the sound of his voice on the phone.

At that time, Dad lived in Donetsk, Ukraine. It was an occupied territory controlled by Russia and a self-proclaimed state called the "DNR – Donetsk People's Republic." There was a war going on. COVID-19 was rampant, hospitals were overwhelmed, and Dad couldn't receive timely medical care. We, his children, tried to help in any way we could. We contacted acquaintances in search of doctors, stayed in constant touch with Dad, and wanted to support him.

I spoke with him only over the phone during his final days and couldn't be by his side, just like my brother and sister couldn't. Thousands of kilometers of military borders separated us from my dad. We couldn't move freely within our country, and our lives were at significant risk, so that we couldn't visit our hometown of Donetsk. This was why we couldn't come and be with our dad in his last days.

I realized things were turning for the worse when my dad stopped joking. What's so significant about that? My dad was a man with an incredible sense of humor. I remember hundreds of jokes he told, and I've forgotten hundreds more. Dad was always the life of the party. His witty remarks and jokes brought joy and laughter to those around him. My friends always told me my dad was a wonderful person with a fantastic sense of humor. I believe his sense of humor was his "life energy." I know this because that energy lives on in his children and grandchildren. There wasn't a day when my dad didn't crack a joke, except for the period after my grandmother's death.

When he stopped joking, I got scared and felt something was wrong. Then, a few days later, my brother Sergey called. He said, "Dad passed away..." with pain in his voice. Once again, that terrible pain, fear, and despair pierced my soul. I sat on the floor, unable to hold back the tears. I couldn't breathe properly, and I cried, staring into emptiness. Those were the worst days of my life after my mom's death.

The official cause of my dad's death was a "detached thrombus." But I have a different opinion. A thrombus is a consequence of blood clotting, and the real cause was COVID-19. It's just that the doctors in the Donetsk People's Republic (DPR) either didn't have the time or couldn't determine that my dad was infected with the deadly virus. The same symptoms my dad had appeared a year later in 2021 and nearly took my life with COVID-19. That period changed my life forever, but we'll talk about that later. I miss my mom and dad so much right now. May they rest in peace! I love you!

My family, who were there with me, helped me get through those dreadful days. My Hanna, our children, my brother and sister, and their families. It was a challenging year for all of us. Due to the war and COVID-19, we couldn't even attend our parents' funerals. And to this day, we haven't been able to visit their graves. Only my brother Sergey managed to go to our dad's funeral and visit our mom's grave. Cursed be this war!

The pain of losing loved ones is indescribable! I hope you never have to experience this feeling. But death is a natural part of life, and we have no choice. Sooner or later, we will all face the loss of our loved ones. Be brave! And remember that your loved ones have not left you forever. Their souls and energy will remain in your Family Tree if you, your children, and your descendants remember them!

Why did I share this pain and these memories? So that you understand the value of losing loved ones! And be grateful to the Universe for every day and moment when your loved ones are with you. Don't waste your time on quarrels, disagreements, relationship issues, and other negative emotions. Spend as much time together as possible. Love and cherish each other. Embrace each other in this life until it's time to say goodbye to this physical embodiment of your loved ones. Thank the Universe for it every day!

Now, let's discuss your Gratitude to the Universe for its gifts. Be grateful to it for material blessings (matter) with which it has endowed you. No matter how materialistic it may sound. You are fortunate if you have a roof over your head, a job, clothing, and food on the table.

Be grateful to the Universe for everything you have right now! This will help you appreciate and preserve your material blessings. Many people on Earth don't have a fraction of what you possess. In this world, so many homeless and hungry people are freezing on the streets. They dream of what seems like trivial and ordinary things that you have. A warm apartment, electricity, clean water, clothing, and food. Thank the Universe for what you have.

Right now, there is a war in Ukraine, and almost every day, urban infrastructure, heating and power plants, residential buildings, and entire cities are being destroyed. Millions of people are left without electricity, water, and heating in their homes. Thousands have also lost their homes. For the Ukrainian people, the second winter has brought a terrifying ordeal. People have come face to face with darkness, cold, and hunger. My brother, sister, family, and friends are now in Ukraine. Every day, I pray to the Universe and ask my ancestors to help them survive all this horror. And I thank it for everything my family has for my everyday life—a roof over our heads, food on the table, warm clothing, and good jobs. We are safe. We can sleep peacefully in silence. Thank you, Universe, for this!

Thank the Universe for those moments when it answers your requests and prayers. You dreamed of a kitten, and now you're petting it in your arms. Thank the Universe! You got a promotion at work. Express your gratitude. You bought a new car. You know what to do. Your children recovered from an illness. You fulfilled a cherished dream. You basked in the sun by the ocean. The Muse visited you, or you experienced a moment of revelation - "Universe, I thank you!"

Gratitude is receiving feedback from the Universe and the material world. Imagine yourself in the place of the Universe. Close your eyes. Around you, you sense a whole world full of objects, sounds, and scents. And then, out of the darkness, comes someone's request. For example, "Universe, I ask you to give me a new smartphone!" You look around. You gather matter and search for a way to create that coveted gadget. You make and bring it into existence. Holding it in your hands, you feel its shape and weight, examining the screen's color palette. And then, you throw that smartphone into the void, in the direction from where the request came. And silence. Did it reach its destination? Was it caught? Maybe it wasn't liked? Or did I create something different from the request? Or did it arrive but end up in the wrong hands? In any case, since there's silence, it means there's no need to respond to these requests because something went wrong.

The conclusion is this: if the Universe grants you what you asked for, give feedback! Thank the Universe because it expended its energy and matter on this request. Let it be heard that everything is fine. That the package has been delivered. That you are delighted with it. And you can continue collaborating. After all, you are very grateful for the gifts from the Universe! Or, at the very least, say, "Oops!" if something arrived unexpectedly. This will also help the Universe receive feedback.

The example is playful and exaggerated, but you've grasped the essence. Be grateful to the Universe for everything it gives you! For it, this is just as important as it is for you. Keep it from reaching the point where the Universe stops responding to your requests and prayers! Thank it! Every day! For all the material things you have and for all the loved ones who are with you right now!

Put the book aside. Go and hug your beloved parents, children, or friends right now. Warm them with your embrace. Spend time with them. Tell them how much you love them and value your time together. And...

"Universe, thank you for everything!"

FAITH

In interacting with the Universe, one of the key roles is played by "Faith." It is a powerful conviction, on par with Love and Gratitude. Faith amplifies the flow of your thoughts and prays into the Universe.

In my understanding, Faith is the process of realizing that what you believe in is an unshakable truth. It means that you are sure of this existence, and you don't need additional proof, arguments, or the beliefs of others to know that it is true.

People believe in many things in this world. In gods, in the existence of afterlife realms, in steadfast love and friendship. Some believe in UFOs, vampires, the conspiracies of the powerful, and ancient cults, or that the boss will increase their salary "right away." Some even believed that the war they started, the killings, and the deaths they spread across the land were sacred to them. And some believe that all the madness humanity creates will eventually end with the triumph of good. We are all inclined to believe in what we want to see in our lives and what should surround us.

Why do superstitions work? Why is a black cat crossing your path considered bad luck? If you break a mirror, are you destined for seven years of misfortune? Or... you can insert a dozen superstitions from your ancestors and cultures. Why do these things work? Because people believe in them! Faith is such a powerful conviction that it can "bring to life" any of your beliefs. That's why these superstitions only work for those who believe in them. But try to stop thinking about them. Will they still come true?

So, how can you harness such a powerful tool as Faith?

You need to realize that Faith, combined with a strong desire, creates a message to the Universe capable of bringing about whatever you wish. It's a powerful but only partially safe tool. If you believe nonconditionally in something, it becomes a part of your Universe. My friend once said, "Be careful with your wishes; they tend to come true." He had wanted to touch up the paint on his car for six months where there were scratches but kept postponing it.

In the end, he got into a severe accident. He survived, but his car was severely damaged and had to be completely repainted. The Universe will always give you what you desire, but only sometimes in the way you want it. Remember this and be cautious with your desires.

If you want something or are praying for something from the Universe, harness your Faith. Drive away all thoughts of doubt from your mind. You must be 100% certain that your desired outcome will come to pass and that the Universe will hear you no matter what.

Once, standing in a church, I pondered, "Why does God hear people better here than in other places?" The answer came to me over time. It's because people in the church possess "greater Faith." Everything that surrounds you in a "house of God" - icons, beautiful frescoes on the walls, vintage windows, the splendid attire of the clergy, their singing - is designed to amplify your Faith in one deity or another. That's why gods hear your prayers better in churches and temples than elsewhere.

And if you think about it, all this power emanates from your body and soul! Take two people who worship different gods, preach other faiths, and pray equally. Now remove all this "divine decor" around them. What remains? What unites them? That's right, only their Faith, thoughts, and words!

Find your path, your "channel" to the Universe. Start praying and having Faith. Faith has changed humanity and the Universe around us. Some people believed the Earth was not flat and discovered the Solar System. Others thought there were more lands beyond the oceans and discovered new continents. Still, others believed in victory and managed to stop wars and the mad rulers who brought chaos and death. Some think that we will become a multi-planetary species and are launching ships into space. We all believe in different things. The main thing is to believe!

Even if the Universe doesn't respond to you here and now, don't give up; keep believing. Send your energetic signals to it. Humanity knows thousands of examples where Faith helps perform miracles when paralyzed individuals start walking again when people escape from seemingly hopeless situations, when good triumphs over evil, and similar incredible events. Faith is the key to solving all these miracles. It is a compelling conviction capable of turning your Universe upside down and transforming it beyond recognition. So, use it! Don't doubt! Believe! And the Universe will surely reward you!

CAUSAL CONNECTIONS

Now, I would like to discuss the concept of "fate" and its influence on our lives. "Did fate bring us together today?" Let's figure it out.

First, let's familiarize ourselves with "causal connections." Any event is a "cause" and leads to inevitable "consequences." In other words, a change in the state of something results in specific outcomes.

Let's consider an example. The alarm clock rang in the morning – that's the cause. You woke up because of it – that's the consequence. If we trace events backward, the alarm clock rang (consequence) because you set it the night before (cause). You put it – that's another consequence. Why did you set it – that's the cause. And so on.

These causal connections can describe any actions and events that occur in the Universe. Every effort has consequences, and every result has a cause.

Thus, a specific sequence of billions of diverse but sequential events in the Universe led to the formation of galaxies, stars, the Solar System, planets, Earth, water, air, plants, animals, and us. You are the consequence of countless causes, including the meeting of your parents, their love, your conception, birth, and all the events that made you who you are.

If we combine all the chains of causal connections into one large chain, we get what is called "life." All these connections have brought us to where we are now. They have determined the appearance of the Universe that we see before us.

If we take a person's life path and place it on a timeline, marking all significant events such as birth, school, university, work, marriage, death, etc., we get a straight line of life. At this point, many would say that this is a person's "fate." Fate guided them through life, marking these key points and more. They had no choice; it was fate!

But imagine that at each of these critical points in the line of life, a person had not just one option but several – in other words, there was a choice of "which path to take." Then, the line of life starts to resemble a tree branch. Call it the "tree of a person's life." You get a different destiny depending on the decision made at each " turning point" in your life.

So, if we consider a person's entire life, their fate consists of a series of choices made at pivotal moments, leading them to the final destination. Why "turning points"? Because they can change the direction of your destiny, so to speak, "alter the course of events." This means that your fate depends solely on your choice! Your life is in your hands. Where and how you will live, what kind of person you will become – it all depends on you and your actions and decisions, not on some imaginary "fate" that left you no choice.

For people incapable of making critical conscious decisions and recognizing pivotal moments, fate becomes an unconscious choice or "going with the flow of life." It's a combination of circumstances you don't want or can't influence, leading you through life – it's the autopilot of the Universe. Such an unconscious life can sometimes be beneficial for the Universe. It can give what is desired to those who live consciously.

If you don't learn to recognize pivotal moments and trust fate, you'll live an unconscious life on autopilot. Most likely, at the end of your life, or perhaps even earlier, you'll start asking questions like, "Why am I married to this person? Why did I study for a profession

I don't want to pursue? Why am I poor? Why am I not happy?" and so on.

To prevent this, start training in mindfulness. When making important decisions, think about different outcomes and future consequences. Learn to take responsibility. Remember, every decision you make (the cause) will lead to results. They can be desirable or not. You will need to learn to be accountable for your choices. This is responsibility for your life.

Do you want to live your life consciously, with excitement and happiness, or will you let "fate" and the Universe control you?

GOALS

"All right," you might say, "I'm ready to take control of my life consciously and navigate my path by making informed decisions. But where should it lead me, and to what?"

As you may have guessed, the answer lies in your Goals. It would be best to learn how to set various goals so that your life's journey is not in vain, and your life is as rich as possible with happiness, enjoyment, and satisfaction.

So, what is a "Goal"? It is something desirable, the result of actions, or a state you want to achieve or be in. For example, you may want to change the world for the better, become famous, become wealthy, be a happy husband and father, be understood by your parents, own a beautiful car, or, as a last resort, have a chocolate cake. All of these are different types of goals.

Here's the good news: everyone has their own goals. There is such a vast variety of them that all of humanity won't find itself in the same final point at the same time when everyone has achieved their goals. The bad news is that many plans will remain unattained by some people due to lack of motivation, laziness, setting goals incorrectly, and so on. But this is terrible news, only for some. I'm confident that you belong to the category of people who will manage to achieve their set goals!

Goals can be of several types: long-term, for an extended period; medium-term, for a short period; short-term, for the minimal time and quick accomplishment. An example of a long-term goal could be your desire to build a family and become a happy parent to three children. In this case, medium-term goals could include finding a suitable partner, family planning, and buying a home for your "family nest." To achieve long-term and medium-term goals, you'll need numerous short-term goals, such as:

- self-improvement to have a more attractive appearance and be an exciting conversationalist.
- visits to restaurants, clubs, cinemas, theatres, and other crowded places to meet new people and find a potential partner for starting a family.
- numerous encounters with the opposite sex and hours of conversation to get to know each other better.
- the "honeymoon" period with romantic dates and pleasant moments spent together.
- getting to know your partner's parents.

- organizing the long-awaited wedding.
- planning and raising offspring.
- earning and saving money for your home.
- raising children with numerous daycare centers, schools, colleges, and universities.
- and so on, and similar goals.

All these short-term goals can be broken down into smaller ones. For instance, organizing a wedding alone involves hundreds of smaller goals that can be classified as "tasks."

From all the above, we can draw the following conclusion: to achieve a long-term goal, you need to break it down into medium-term ones, and they, in turn, into smaller short-term goals. Keep doing this until you have a specific "to-do list" for each purpose. Yes, it's precisely a to-do list. You must clearly understand in which period, with what result, and specific steps you should take to achieve your goals. For this purpose, a detailed list of tasks with the specified timing of their completion and expected results is most suitable.

For example, my long-term goal was to "find a safe and optimal place for my family and our future descendants to live." About ten years ago, when I started thinking about my family's safety, I set this goal myself. I began breaking it down into medium-term and smaller goals, asking myself questions to achieve them. What place on Earth can be safe, free from natural disasters, with a suitable climate for us if we don't consider national borders? What stable and economically developed countries are located in these territories? What are the current economic indicators and prospects for these countries? What nuances exist in obtaining citizenship and learning the state language in these countries? How can I migrate there? What profession is needed to find a job and quickly adapt to a new land? Where will it be safe to raise children and live peacefully?

There were numerous questions. I studied our planet, countries, professions, migration methods, etc. After researching a vast amount of diverse information, I realized that no ideal place on Earth exists. Everywhere has its nuances, advantages, disadvantages, and pitfalls. So, I began to look for the optimal solution. I focused on the pros that were important to me. I examined the cons and decided whether to accept them to achieve a more critical goal.

My choice fell in Canada. I'm not claiming that it's a perfect country in all respects, but personally, it became the number one choice for many factors. "Great," I thought, "now I have a long-term goal – to migrate to Canada!" What do I need for that?

Next, I started breaking down this long-term goal into smaller components. What do I need to do to migrate to Canada? Gathering the necessary information, analyzing it, and reflecting on it, I came up with a list of the following goals:

- Learn English as a family.
- Save up a sufficient amount of money.

- Acquire a new, more versatile profession.
- Study the methods of migration and citizenship acquisition, and so on.

These goals were broken down into many smaller goals. For example, the purpose of "learning English" was broken down into:

- Taking lessons with a tutor.
- Improving all aspects of the language: reading, writing, listening, speaking.
- Finding a job where English is spoken.

This list, in turn, generated new goals:

- Finding a tutor.
- Finding books and courses for language learning.
- Finding websites for communicating with native speakers.
- Creating a study plan.

To achieve these goals, I began to create lists of tasks, such as:

1. Finding contacts for tutors in our area on the Internet.
2. Calling all contacts and inquiring about course schedules and prices. Are there any available slots?
3. Deciding on a tutor and arranging lessons.
4. Creating a study plan and coordinating it with my schedule.
5. Purchasing all the necessary supplies: stationery, books, etc.
6. Planning the route to the tutor and calculating the travel time, among other things.

The more specific your action plan is, the more likely you are to achieve your goal with the desired results and within the set time frames. You need concrete steps that are as detailed as possible. Dedicate enough time and effort to this, as it is essential. Ultimately, you will obtain a clear "action guide" and an "instruction manual for achieving your goal." This will allow you to move toward your intended destination in small steps!

Understanding that these goals and tasks are not set in stone is essential. You can and should modify them as needed! My initial list could have been better. I constantly adapted and changed it. Yes, after ten years, I now live in Canada. However, it was a challenging journey, and my initial goals changed many times. I adapted them to the circumstances. I even had the opportunity to live in another country before reaching Canada. Learning English continues even now. I changed my profession five years after the initial plan, but for different reasons, and it worked out for the best. The migration process turned out to be completely different as well. While I was planning one route, Canada offered us a unique opportunity to migrate through another new program for assisting Ukrainians. Thank you, Canada!

You and only you create the list of your goals and tasks. So why not change or update it if necessary? In the end, the important thing is to achieve your goal! It's like embarking on a long journey by car with a navigator. You select the starting and ending points of your trip. The navigator devises a tentative route with intermediate stops. You confirm it and set out on your way!

What is the likelihood that everything will go as planned and missed a turn? No problem. The navigator will recalculate the route. Forgot your favorite sweater? Buy a new one. Have you had a flat tire? You know what to do! The key is to keep moving forward. Adjust your plan and adapt to new circumstances. Then, you will undoubtedly reach your goal!

It took me about ten years to achieve my main long-term goal! It required a lot of energy, time, and effort, but it was worth it! I experienced incredible satisfaction from completing the task and achieving the set goal! You will also enjoy that feeling!

I achieved my main long-term goal. What am I busy with now? I created a new list of my long-term, medium-term, and short-term goals. One of them is to finish working on this book and publish it. I want to convey my ideas about the existence and importance of Life in the Universe to as many readers as possible. I hope this goal will be realized shortly. It's essential not only for me and my family but for you and humanity. I want to see as many kinds, of conscious, rational, intelligent, and happy people as possible.

* * *

Great! We've understood how to break down long-term goals into smaller ones and create task lists. But how do you choose the right destination? What should it be like to be worth the effort you're going to invest in it? After all, you're planning to dedicate a significant amount of time and effort to it, and the last thing you want is to discover at the end of the road that you are heading for the wrong goal. This can be disheartening and discouraging. So, it's essential to carefully choose the endpoint of one of your most significant life journeys.

How can you do that? You need to listen to your desires and your inner voice. Find something that will make you happy. Ask yourself, "What is my number one priority, and what truly matters to me? What will genuinely make me happy? What goal is worth all the effort I plan to put in over the coming days, months, and years?"

Remember, only you can answer these questions! Listen to your intuition and your inner voice. Find your genuine desire. Discard anything that has been imposed by others or society. This goal must make you happy. That will be your best motivation! Choose carefully and responsibly so that the result doesn't disappoint you in the future.

The Universe has given humanity the freedom of choice. It has allowed you to choose a goal for your entire life. You can and should take advantage of this! Look within yourself. Ask your soul what it desires and how it wants to live this life. Find the answers. They will become your life goals.

There is another crucial element in your life that you must discover—your "life purpose." It's the primary mission or assignment that the Universe has prepared for you. It's the "life lesson" your soul must undergo.

Why does the Universe need purposes? Remember how it orchestrates life? It has its "grand design" and development plan. Therefore, the Universe gives us particular tasks to ensure that humanity moves forward and evolves. Each person contributes to the development of the Universe by fulfilling their specific purpose.

The Universe prepares entirely different purposes for each of us. For example, your calling might be to create a musical composition that inspires people. Or it could be to be a great father to your son, who, in turn, becomes a great leader of your nation. You may need to build a magnificent building or architectural monument symbolizing freedom. Or you might need to gather valuable information from various sources and then pass on that wisdom to future generations as a book. Maybe your destiny is to invent a cure for cancer. Or you'll revolutionize the energy industry with electric cars and create a self-sustaining colony on Mars. Your purpose will always be unique. It may not always be "great," but it's definitely "significant"! You may have more than one call, but you have one!

Considering it's essential, how do you find or understand your life purpose? First, you must listen to yourself, your desires and talents. You must ask yourself, "What valuable and meaningful thing can I do to improve the world? How can I be useful to my family, loved ones, humanity, and life?" The answers to these questions can serve as a starting point in the search for your purpose.

Secondly, the Universe may sometimes provide hints about your calling. These hints can be challenging to notice and recognize. Pay attention to unusual things happening to you. Listen to your intuition. Most likely, there will come a moment when you have an "aha" moment and realize what the Universe has prepared as your purpose.

I can't predict exactly when this "miracle" will happen to you. But I can confidently say that if you seek it and ask the Universe for it, that moment will undoubtedly come in your life. Let's remember Isaac Newton. His purpose was to become a prominent physicist and describe the three laws of mechanics and the law of universal gravitation. Perhaps he wasn't even aware of it, but the Universe helped him and dropped a famous apple from the tree while resting beneath it. This prompted him to think that all bodies are attracted to each other. Newton's laws changed the course of scientific progress and human history. And it all began with the Universe's subtle yet significant hint.

If you didn't notice the Universe's hints or ignored them and couldn't find the answers within yourself, the Universe may reveal your purpose through revelations or enlightenment. We'll talk about that a little later. Be patient. It's worth it. For example, I discovered my purpose through a revelation from the Universe. It was an unforgettable experience! But more on that later.

It's also important to note that you may choose to avoid following your purpose. Many people never find it throughout their lives. Therefore, the Universe may assign the same mission to different people in different corners of the Earth and at other times to achieve the desired result. But aimless existence won't make you happy. So, if you ever feel that you haven't found your "great goal," think about it and look around. Perhaps your purpose is more straightforward than that of people who change the course of history or create artistic masterpieces. Maybe it involves giving birth to and nurturing that "exceptional person" ? Perhaps you're the happy mother or caring father of the next Einstein ?

As children, we intuitively choose activities that bring us joy. Unfortunately, we often forget this in adulthood. Look back at your childhood; there are clues and answers there. What did you dream of becoming? What brought you real happiness? What pleased your soul?

Feel free to seek your purpose; don't worry about its scale. Remember, the Universe has a "complete picture" and a "global plan." Your puzzle piece may not be as crucial as others, but the whole picture can only be complete without it!

Suppose you've found and understood your purpose; put in the maximum effort to fulfill it! This is essential for the Universe, humanity, and life itself. Make your purpose your number one long-term goal. And from there, you already know what to do with that goal.

* * *

I'm glad to see your enthusiasm for "vision boards" and visualization! These are indeed powerful tools that can help you achieve your goals. Let's dive into them step by step.

A vision board is typically a board or a large sheet of paper with pictures printed, cut out, and pasted onto it that represent your desires and goals. Creating one is easy. You select an image for each wish, print it, cut it out, and glue it onto your vision board. You can find many recommendations and techniques for creating vision boards online. You'll indeed find something that resonates with you. The main principle is to find an image that vividly represents each desire. This is so you can form a clear mental picture of what you want when you look at your vision board. For example, it could be the house of your dreams.

My beloved wife Hanna and I chose a nine-square-sector format for our vision board. Each sector corresponds to a specific area of life and is denoted by its color. In the center, we always glue a photo of our family, as that's the primary purpose of our lives. Around the family photo, we arrange the other eight sectors (starting from the upper left corner and going clockwise around the center):

1. "Wealth" - violet.
2. "Fame, recognition" - red.
3. "Love, relationships" - pink.
4. "Children and creativity" - white.
5. "Travel" - gold.

6. "Work, career" - blue.
7. "Wisdom, knowledge" - orange or brown.
8. "Family" - green.

The colors and names provide only a general idea. If you prefer different colors or want to arrange the sections differently, feel free to do so. This is your vision board, and you should enjoy looking at it every day. So, make it as visually appealing as possible.

We found this example on the internet in image search results. We were drawn to the structure and order in this vision board format. Plus, the presence of different sectors and colors added vibrancy and mood. This vision board worked quite well for us the first time, so we continued to use the same format in the following years.

You can choose any other type of vision board for yourself. Look for examples and techniques for creating one on the internet. Choose what resonates with your soul. You must enjoy looking at the board, receive an energy boost, feel happy, and be inspired to achieve these goals!

In each sector, we glue many small photos representing our desires. We use a collage-making program to create square collages for each section. The images can be specific or abstract, conveying the idea. For example, you can find a picture of your dream house or even go and take a photo of it to have a clear image in your mind. Or you can glue abstract heart images to meet your significant other.

2018, our vision board featured a baby boy in the "Children" sector. In 2019, our son was born. On the following vision board, in the "Education" sector, we added a photo of our little boy underwater. We wanted him to be a good swimmer. And what do you think? Our Lev is as comfortable in the water as a fish. He loves bathing, splashing in all water containers, and taking several baths daily. We go to the pool several times a week for lessons with a trainer and just for swimming. Lev loves water so much that I call him "Aqua Man." So, choose the images that resonate with you. Let them vividly represent your desires. This will help them come true, and your goals will become a reality.

We also specifically described our goals and desires on the reverse side of the vision board. This is done to create a clear mental image of what you desire. When expressing your desires, it's essential to use the present tense, as if you already have it, you've achieved the goal, and the wish has come true. 'We have bought our dream home in (mention the city). It's new, spacious, and cozy...' The more precise the description, the better.

We usually create a new vision board at the end of the current year with our desires and goals for the following year. This helps us refine our goals, review our desires, cross off those that have already come true, and add new ones instead of those that haven't. Yes, sometimes, some wishes don't come true. This depends on various factors—your efforts, life circumstances, the relevance of the goal, and so on. It's not critical; replace that desire with a new one. Onward to achieving them!

Visualization is another crucial part of the process. Congratulations, you've done a great job! You admire your creation—your vision board—full of colorful images, clear descriptions of your desires, and high hopes for their realization. Now, hang this vision board where you can see it daily, like in your bedroom near your bed or above your workspace. Then, start practicing the "magic of visualization."

The secret of visualization is that you should look at your vision board every day or whenever it's convenient and imagine that you've already received what you desire and achieved your goals. This process is called visualization.

The better you can vividly imagine your desires, the easier it is to visualize them, and the more precise your signal to the Universe will be. For example, if there's a picture of a beach in your vision board's "Travel" sector, start visualizing it as if you're already there. Imagine the pristine sandy shore washed by the gentle waves of a clear blue sea, seamlessly merging into the cloudless sky. The bright sun lightly blinds you. A bamboo lounge chair and a rainbow-colored coconut cocktail are calling you. You smile widely and continue visualizing.

Getting comfortable on the lounge chair, you sip your delicious cocktail. Palm leaves create an excellent shade and an unusual pattern for your future tan. A salty breeze runs over your skin, and your soul fills with peace and tranquility.

Keep visualizing all the sensations and emotions as if you're already there. This process will reinforce your desires and goals and send a clear message to the Universe.

Keep in mind that this is an ongoing process. The more consistently and vividly you practice visualization, the more effective it becomes. Over time, you'll find that your desires and goals start manifesting in your life.

So, keep up with your vision board and visualization, and may all your dreams and goals become a reality!

Feel it all! Sense the scent of the sea breeze. Feel the coconut with the cocktail in your hand, every hair that touches your fingers. Taste the sweet flavor of the drink on your lips. Let the slightly firm lounger slats embrace your back. Feel how the gentle sun leaves a tan on your skin. Experience the inner bliss and happiness from all this ecstasy!

You must visualize your desire as if experiencing it in reality, here and now. Engage all your senses and imagination. This is not only a gratifying process but also a highly productive one. By creating clear mental images, you are forming the necessary thoughts and brainwaves to meet the Universe. This way, you communicate what you desire and aspire to achieve it. By sending such signals daily, you amplify your requests manifold. It works like a snowball effect. And when the Universe knows what you want, it can make it happen. It's like a genie from Aladdin's lamp. It will say, "As you wish!", snap its fingers, and fulfill your desire. This is where the true power of visualization lies.

If we look at visualization from the perspective of how the brain works, the process appears as follows. When you have formed a clear image of your desire on paper, described it, and then visualized it repeatedly, a solid neural connection with the idea of your goal is established in your mind. It serves as a target filter for incoming information. Information coming from various sources will be sorted based on these multiple filters. For example, you may accidentally notice a brochure with a colorful picture like your dream on a small table in a business center. Processing these signals, your brain will recognize the similarity with the target filter and tell you, "Hey, wait! It seems this is what we're looking for."

Even if you see this brochure out of the corner of your eye, it will still catch your attention. You will pause for a moment and contemplate. You'll approach to take a closer look, reach out, pick it up, and read its contents. "Awesome! This is what I need!" will resound in your mind when you read the terms of the travel agency's brochure about a trip to paradise islands. Your eyes will light up, and you'll rush towards your dream!

That's how it works. When you articulate your desires, your brain forms target filters and, with their help, helps you find the right image in the general flow of information and catch everything necessary. Your brain will let all the other "noise" pass by and not even pay attention to it. But everything related to your goals and desires will be set aside and marked as "important."

This way, you will receive information about the desired object, find leads, and paths to achieve your goals. Everything that can help you achieve these goals will be accessible to you. All that remains is to process all the information and start acting. And where will all these circumstances, people, situations, and coincidences on your life's journey come from? Remember, the Universe always responds: "As you wish! Your desire is law to me!" It will find a way to guide you along the right path.

I first learned about "visualization" from the enlightening and motivating film "The Secret" (2006). It turned my consciousness upside down and created a new worldview. The examples and techniques described in it are still something I use to this day, but back then, it was just the beginning of my journey. If you have not seen this film, find it online and dedicate a few hours. The time spent watching it is well worth it!

At a particular stage of my life, I had a goal - to work at one of the best commercial banks in Ukraine. The bank's main office was located near Central Park in Donetsk. It was a standalone, beautiful business building that harmonized perfectly with the local architecture and lake and complemented the park's landscape. Majestic steps led to the central entrance of the building. After passing through the automatic doors, bank employees and clients entered a vast hall with an open space that rose through all the floors to the roof, where a winter garden was located. The building seemed to float around you. The panoramic elevator inside the hall added movement to this harmony. The bank's staff were always friendly and smiling. It was my dream job at that time.

I gathered the necessary information about the bank online, and I also asked several fellow students from the university who worked there. I decided for myself that this was the place where I wanted to work. At that time, I was working at the National Bank of Ukraine (NBU). It was a state bank responsible for supervising the banking market and overseeing commercial banks. I worked there in the department responsible for the electronic payment system within the country. The job was fascinating, but I felt stuck in one place and began to look for something new. I wanted career growth and change in my life.

After watching the movie "The Secret," I decided to test whether visualization works and works for me. I started visualizing myself working at the bank of my dreams. With my eyes closed, I imagined going to work in the morning. Dressed in a sharp black business suit, carrying a briefcase, and wearing polished, shiny black shoes, I confidently climbed the steps. Upon entering the building's lobby, important people greeted me and shook my hand. With a smile and a confident stride, I joined the panoramic elevator and began to conquer new heights at my dream job!

Every time I had a spare moment, I tried to visualize this image in my mind. I repeated it over and over for several months. I found it interesting to conduct this mental experiment. I also liked the vision I had created. Perhaps deep down in my "skeptical" brain, I wanted to prove that the idea of visualization "lacked any scientific basis and certainly wouldn't work."

That was the case until one day when an ordinary, unremarkable phone call rang out. I receive dozens of calls like that every day from various banks. It was part of my job to help commercial banks deal with the intricacies of the national electronic payment system. On the other end of the line, a guy introduced himself on behalf of the bank I had dreamt of working at. We discussed work-related matters. After a short pause, the voice on the other end of the phone asked, "Chudov, is this you?"

To my surprise, it was Egor - my classmate from university. We had been in the same class. I knew he worked at the bank of my dreams, but I hadn't discussed his work with him until this phone call. Egor recognized me. I was pleasantly surprised to hear his voice. We chatted briefly about life and shared funny memories of our university days. He inquired about what I was doing at the NBU and said, "Would you like to work with us at our bank?"

Several months and a couple of interviews later, I landed the job at the bank of my dreams. I worked there with Egor for over eight years. We became friends. I met many wonderful people in the bank, made new friends, grew professionally, and had an unforgettable time. Thanks to this job, in 2014, when the war started in Donetsk, my family and I could move to Kyiv, the capital of Ukraine. The position of my dreams changed the course of events in my life, protected my family from the war, and helped us find a new home.

So, goal visualization helped me "randomly" land my dream job and change my life! Since then, I have used this technique often, and it always works. Visualization, patience, and a sprinkle of faith in the power of the Universe can materialize all your desires!

Create a vision board for yourself. Visualize every day. And remember – all wishes come true because the Universe always says, "As you wish!"

* * *

For me, a vivid example of setting and achieving long-term goals correctly has been the achievements of Elon Musk. This remarkable and somewhat eccentric individual is one of our time's greatest minds, engineers, and entrepreneurs. I have been following his successes and failures for many years. My initial interest in Musk and his company, Tesla, began around 2010 with the launch of the first Tesla Roadster model. Later, I became intrigued by his new space company, SpaceX. I remember his interviews and presentations over the subsequent years, where he outlined his long-term goals: transitioning humanity to electric vehicles and sustainable renewable energy, creating reusable rockets, and establishing a self-sustaining colony on Mars.

At that time, these goals seemed unreal. How could humanity switch to electric vehicles in a world dominated by oil magnates and corporations? Ha, Elon Musk had almost no chance! Was he making a reusable rocket for Mars missions using the resources of his private company, SpaceX? Ha-ha-ha, even NASA wasn't taking on goals that ambitious! It bordered on madness!

But something told me that a dreamer at heart and an engineer in mind, like Musk, could achieve specific successes. Curiosity got the better of me, and I began to observe him, his accomplishments, failures, and incredible work ethic. What did he do? Right. He defined long-term goals, broke them down into medium-term and short-term objectives, made task lists, and started working on one task after another. He assembled an incredibly talented and hardworking team around him. Elon Musk began with small jobs and moved step by step toward his success.

Today, Tesla and SpaceX are known worldwide. Under Elon Musk's leadership, Tesla has accomplished an incredible feat and now produces nearly a million electric vehicles globally yearly. They've revolutionized the automobile industry. Today, almost every global automaker has announced plans to phase out gasoline-powered cars in the next ten to fifteen years. This is the influence and triumph of Tesla! But these changes will benefit humanity for many years if not millennia. Musk's genius has changed the world for the better, no matter how "loud" that may sound.

SpaceX, in turn, has achieved something incredible at first glance. They managed to make the first stage of a rocket reusable. They learned how to return it to Earth and use it again! The entire rocket industry had previously assumed that most of a rocket was disposable and couldn't be returned to Earth for reuse. But SpaceX did it!

I watched the first successful rocket landing live. It was an incredible sight! My heart felt like it was trying to break free from my chest. I got a second of the broadcast. The countdown began: 10, 9, 8... liftoff! Billowing smoke, flames, the roar of engines, and the rocket soared into the sky. After a few minutes, the first stage separated and returned to Earth. The whole world held its breath. The time I slowed down. Everyone was on edge.

Could SpaceX land the rocket? Would it be a long-awaited success or another failure? The rocket's first stage deployed its landing legs and ignited its engines. The Earth grew closer and closer. A cry of joy erupted from me. He did it! It was unbelievable! The rocket stood on the landing pad as if it had never left. Yes, as confidently as if SpaceX landed rockets every day. This monumental event changed the rocket industry forever.

And that was just one of Elon Musk's medium-term goals for SpaceX. Today, the company conducts dozens of launches annually and successfully retrieves nearly all the rocket stages. They've designed and launched the Falcon Heavy, a heavy-lift rocket with two boosters. My whole family watched the first launch. The synchronized landing of the two boosters will remain one of our most vivid memories. Later, Musk sent the first all-civilian crew of four into orbit. Just imagine ordinary people, not astronauts, venturing into space! And more teams followed. SpaceX also deployed hundreds of its Starlink satellites into orbit to provide wireless internet coverage for Earth.

SpaceX's next long-term goal is to launch the Starship, a fully reusable rocket. The first rockets of this type are being assembled and tested at Starbase. These are the most enormous rockets in the world, capable of carrying dozens of people and hundreds of tons of cargo into orbit and even travelling to the Moon and Mars. Musk's company has already secured a contract from NASA to deliver cargo for constructing the first lunar base. After several years of successful launches, we will likely witness the first Starship flight to Mars. Just thinking about this makes my head spin, takes my breath away, and fills me with excitement. That will be a spectacle!

Elon Musk has proven with his hard work and determination that you can solve any engineering problem, create incredible technologies, and change the world for the better. He has established many successful companies that will undoubtedly alter the course of technological development and everyday life for humanity. Personally, Elon Musk has become an example for me to follow!

Now, you and I know you can achieve any goal you set if you choose wisely and consistently work toward it. Elon Musk did it, I did it, and you can too!

Interestingly, what would have happened if I had chosen "a moon landing" as my long-term goal ten years ago? Could I have succeeded then? Nobody will ever know. But you should certainly select your next long-term goal more carefully. After all, you will undoubtedly achieve it!

As a homework assignment, create a list of goals for yourself. Determine your main long-term goal. Break it down into intermediate goals and then into short-term goals. Create detailed task lists. Describe everything in as much detail as possible.

The next step is to create a vision board. This process is fascinating. Get a dose of positive emotions. Specify your goals and desires visually and in writing. Hang all this beauty on the wall in the most visible place. Start visualizing as often as possible.

Set the book aside briefly and do it! Involve the whole family! Be creative and dream! Enjoy this process!

And be sure to come back to finish reading the book. There is still much to discuss. For example, what to do next with the list of goals and tasks, the vision board, and visualizations? Is this the entire formula for success?

ACTION

So, you've defined your long-term, intermediate, and short-term goals and created clear task lists. The visualization board adorns your wall, and your thoughts are floating in vibrant visualization images. What to do next? It's simple—ACT! Yes, in capital letters! Action is the key to achieving your goals!

Let's solve a riddle: "Three birds were sitting on a tree. The first one dreamed of flying to warm lands, the second one wanted to fly away, and the third one set a goal to fly away. How many birds are left sitting in the tree?" You've probably guessed it already. The correct answer is that all three birds are still sitting in the tree! Yes, all three. Because merely dreaming, passionately wishing, or having a clear goal is not enough. To fly, you need to flap your wings and take off, continuing until you achieve the desired result. You need to act!

If you think about something and want to obtain it, those are your dreams or desires. On their own, they don't come true. You've probably tried making hundreds of wishes on birthdays New Year's, and performed various beautiful and slightly mystical rituals, and nothing works.

For example, my parents had a special New Year's ritual: as the clock struck midnight, they had to write their wishes on small pieces of paper quickly. Then, they would set them on fire, wait for them to burn, and toss the remaining ashes into a glass of champagne. And, of course, they had to finish drinking it. As children, we always had huge smiles watching the adults rush through this ritual. I hope that at least some of their wishes come true. Otherwise, they were drinking champagne with paper ashes.

Humanity has created hundreds, maybe even thousands, of such rituals, all aimed at clarifying one's desires and believing in their fulfillment. But as you already know, even with firm belief and conviction, you still need to transform your desires into goals and task lists.

The next step is to act! You can spend years thinking about your goals and looking at your task lists, but if you do nothing, your goals will remain dreams and wishes. It's the combination of having a plan and taking action that distinguishes a project from an achieved result. Here's a simple formula:

Goal + Action = Result

Why do goals plus action lead to results? Because without action, a plan is just a dream. And action with a plan is a good use of energy and time. The combination of a goal and action will deliver the desired result!

To start acting, you need to take one step. Something small from your task list. But it's crucial to take that first step, then another, and another. Like a child learning to walk, you'll move toward your goal step by step.

Yes, you'll encounter obstacles along the way. You'll fall. Other people will encourage you to move forward. There will be challenges. What sets apart a successful person who reaches their goals from others is the ability to keep moving forward no matter what.

Professional boxers are a perfect example. How much energy and effort do they put into training? How often do they get hit in the head and body? How much blood is shed, brows cut, and faces bruised? How many times do they get knocked out? All of this for one goal—to win a championship belt. How many times could they have given up, quit their training, and not get up from the ring floor? But persistence and determination make them get up and move forward every time!

This applies to any successful person, whether an athlete, musician, entrepreneur, chef, builder or a mother raising children.

They all follow the same formula: "Goal + Action = Result." If they can do it, then you can too!

Once, as a teenager, I realized a simple truth:

"If one person can do something, I can repeat it!"

This realization came to me after I saw an incredible story on television. They talked about a young woman and her child in a short interview. The mother and her baby were sitting on the floor. She was talking about the challenges of being a young mother, but her eyes were filled with happiness when she looked at her child. Then, they showed how she fed the baby with a spoon, changed diapers, played with him, and so on. Millions of mothers around the world do the same things every day.

The reporter didn't say much; he couldn't take his eyes off the mother and the baby. At some point, he froze in astonishment. He looked like a marble statue, frozen without movement. Probably at that moment, I examined the same from the outside. I experienced shock and inspiration that still follow me to this day. It was a caring, loving mother who cared for her baby—with her feet. She had no arms! Everything she did—feeding, diapering, playing, etc.—she did with her feet! It was astonishing! She never gave up and didn't stop at anything in her pursuit of becoming a good mother! She became my hero!

At that moment, I realized one thing – if she could achieve the impossible, I, a healthy young man, could accomplish anything, too! And there are thousands of such inspiring stories in human history. People do incredible things despite being limited in their abilities. And it's awe-inspiring, unique, and truly inspirational! From then on, I had no more excuses or reasons not to do something. I know that I can do anything! The only limitation could be my genetically determined potential, but even then, not in all cases, as we've seen.

You only need a goal, theory, practice, and regular actions to achieve results. Your determination, belief in success, and positive attitude will give you an excellent start. To do something, you first need to understand how to do it. This is where theory comes in. Before any action, you must explain how it should be done to your brain. By mentally rehearsing the instructions, your brain forms stable neural connections for future use.

The operation of neurons in your brain during the visualization of actions and their execution hardly differs. This means you can learn to safely perform any action in a "virtual environment" before doing it. For example, in preparing athletes for the Olympic Games, coaches would instruct athletes to visualize themselves successfully running their distance in their minds. Medical personnel measured athletes' brain activity during both visualization and actual running. The brain activity was nearly identical in both scenarios. Take advantage of this. Train your brain to perform a task in your imagination before executing it.

To achieve any result, actions and regular practice are equally important. The more training you have, the stronger the neural connections in your brain, and the better you become at any action, becoming a professional in your field.

Several rules for each stage help me and will help you in achieving goals and getting results:

1) *The goal* must be clearly defined and have a time limit, i.e., a "deadline" - a specific date by which you must complete your task.

2) *Theoretical knowledge* should be gathered from various sources. In the modern world of freely available information, we have access to an unlimited flow of knowledge, but not all of it is reliable and accurately describes the truth. This information stream has a lot of unnecessary and distracting noise. Therefore, I recommend using at least three to ten different sources as a foundation to reach the truth. Please familiarize yourself with the information and identify what they have in common; this will be your theoretical knowledge base, your truth.

3) *Action* should be urgent. There is the "72-hour rule" by Bodo Schaefer, a well-known financial consultant, writer, business trainer, and time management expert. His rule states, "If you have a goal or an idea, you must take the first step within 72 hours (three days) to achieve it. Otherwise, there is a high probability that you will never realize it." The rule works excellently for me as the initial stimulus. Starting with something small is essential, but you must begin to. Then, you remember the idea, dedicate more time to it, think about it more often, and, most importantly, act.

4) *Regular, thoughtful actions* are the path to your goal. The difference between professionals and amateurs in any field is the quality of practice they put in. It varies for everyone. But undoubtedly, you need to put in many hours of strenuous work to achieve significant results. It doesn't matter how much work you do at once. What matters is how often and for how long you keep doing it. Each day will differ from the previous one regarding your emotional and energetic state and external circumstances. Therefore, achieving the same result with the same work will be challenging. But it's crucial to keep going, no matter what. Always continue moving forward. Sooner or later, you will reach your destination. And your actions need to be well thought out and controlled by you. This will increase their productivity many times over.

5) Analyze *final and intermediate results* regularly. My dad once taught me a simple rule: "Every evening, before going to bed, recall what you accomplished during the day, and you'll know if you lived it to the fullest." This is excellent practice! It always motivates me to do something every day and helps me analyze if I'm heading in the right direction and at the right pace.

These simple rules and techniques will help you achieve your goals. It's essential to start and keep acting, relying on this foundation. Beyond that, develop your measures, explore new things, and conquer new heights!

"But sometimes I'm so lazy!" you might say. And you'd be right! I, too, sometimes feel reluctant to start or continue something old.

You're not alone; there are about eight billion of us! Yes, I'm sure laziness is an integral part of every person. It's related to the structure of our bodies.

Laziness is the energy-saving mode of our biological shell. Our bodies accumulate energy for a long time and are reluctant to part with it. We must "hunt the mammoth" for several days and then spend hours hunting it. If we manage to survive the battle with the enormous beast, a lot more time goes into butchering the carcass, obtaining fire, and preparing food. Finally, after gnawing the last bone, we settled comfortably on a new hide and switched to energy-saving mode. At that very moment, our spouse asks us to "wash the dishes." And that's when Laziness kicks in. After all, hunting the mammoth took so much of our energy.

I'm, of course, exaggerating, and no one hunts mammoths in our time. Our hunting now boils down to a trip to the store and choosing ready-made products from the shelves. But nowadays, we have a thousand other things that consume our energy every day: work, sports, taking care of children, household chores, hobbies, and so on. Replenishing lost energy is only sometimes quick and complete. That's when our brain activates its energy-saving mode at every convenient opportunity, and we become lazy.

Everyone is familiar with the feeling of laziness, including you. We want to laze in bed a little longer in the morning; our actions are unreasonably slow; we find a thousand and one reasons not to do what needs to be done. We don't want to tackle complex tasks, sports, work, or household chores, mainly when more exciting and less taxing activities occur. Things like social media, cat videos, computer games, movies, and TV series. Anything that doesn't require leaving your comfortable spot becomes a substitute for natural and essential tasks. That's your laziness.

Laziness hinders any action. It's crucial to recognize it in time, overcome these impulses within yourself, and start acting. To defeat laziness, you need to find a way to increase your energy reserves. This requires proper balanced nutrition and "light exercise" that keeps your biological shell in good shape but doesn't harm it. It would be best to have solid, complete, and quality sleep. Any transformation in your body occurs during periods of rest and recovery. You also need activities that bring joy, pleasure, and happiness. They will boost your internal energy and give you a dose of vitality for the entire day.

The good news is that working at 100% capacity all day is impossible. Our bodies quickly deplete their resources and can malfunction in the form of illnesses, depression, and apathy when we don't want to do anything. So, it's essential to let laziness win occasionally. But it would be best if you did it under your strict control. Learn to listen to your body. Your body knows better when it's efficient to work and when to rest. Only you can determine this. Don't forget to occasionally give yourself a "kick in the rear" to overcome periods of unjustified laziness.

You might argue that you "don't have time." If you do some simple calculations, you'll see that time is limited. On average, a person lives for 70 years. Suppose we subtract the first 20 years of carefree childhood and youth when you don't seriously consider anything and the last 10 years of old age when you won't be able to make grand plans. In that case, you're left with about 40 years of adult, conscious life when you can set and achieve ambitious goals. However, if we subtract one-third of that time for sleep and another third for work that sustains your existence, you're left with approximately 13 years. And if you further deduct time for family, household chores, and basic needs, you're left with "clean" 5-10 years out of your entire life to accomplish your goals and do something significant.

What will you spend your remaining "clean" time on? Social media? Movies and TV series? Engaging books? Video games? Watching videos? Countless entertainment channels will compete for your free time, aiming to profit from you. As a result, you'll have hardly any time left for "great deeds."

"What should I do then?" you might ask. Find something that's worth your remaining hours of free time. Something grand and significant! Learn something new and keep evolving continuously. No time? Do it at night, on weekends, on holidays, and even during your vacation. Find a job in that field so that most of your day is dedicated to achieving your goals. The key is to remember that when you choose what to do in your free time, think about your "great goal" and start acting towards its attainment, regardless of the temptation to get distracted by media content and relax. Mindfulness and self-control are your allies in this challenging battle against laziness and distractions!

Another essential component for achieving your goals is "leveraging." A lever is any tool, knowledge, environment, or object that can simplify or accelerate an action.

To assist you, humanity has invented numerous levers we use daily. Can't move a large rock? Create a lever from a stick and a smaller stone. Don't feel like washing the dishes? Buy a dishwasher. Are you struggling to drive nails into the wall by hand? Use a hammer. Does it take hours to go grocery shopping? Get in your car. Need help to accomplish a task? Assemble a team of professionals in that field around you. Anything that can help you in some way is a lever.

Remember, in any task, you can apply a lever. If it's not readily available, find it. The time spent searching for a lever will make your future work more accessible and compensate for your efforts many times over. If the right lever doesn't exist, invent it! Congratulations, you've come up with an excellent idea. Thanks to it, you can become wealthy and make your work easier for yourself and millions of others. Before starting any action, ask yourself: "What levers can I use to simplify and improve my work?" Choose the right levers and act!

My journey to becoming a software developer exemplifies significant efforts and quality actions. As you already know, I studied this profession at university. However, I didn't work in this field for nearly ten years. When a pivotal moment in my life arrived, I formulated the following goal for myself: to qualify as a developer.

The goal was broken down into short-term objectives. I created plans and task lists and started acting.

Did laziness overcome me? Oh yes, almost every day! But the motivation to "survive and provide for my family" pulverized that laziness. I acted every day for a year and a half until I received my first job offer as a programmer. I delved into a programming language I was new to - Java. I immersed myself in theory and tackled numerous practical tasks. I read dozens of books and countless online articles and completed several online and one extensive offline course.

I learned in any spare moment: sometimes during lunch breaks at work, in the evenings after work, on weekends, holidays, and even on vacation. I knew I would only do this work and achieve the set goal. Given the situation, circumstances, and time available, I acted as efficiently as possible. Of course, I didn't work 24 hours a day, seven days a week, but I aimed to make the most effective use of my time and resources.

Was it worth dedicating a year and a half to this endeavor? Yes! It turned my whole life around! I began to live a life of abundance, relocated my family to a safe place, and engaged in exciting work. Was it a lot for just a year and a half? Receiving the first job offer was only the first step! Over the following seven years, I have always continued learning and exploring new aspects of my profession. I learned and acted at different paces, but the process continues. I strive to learn something new and tackle at least a few priority and non-priority tasks daily.

Life is all about movement! Movement and action! Remember, the only thing distinguishing successful people from everyone else is that they managed to conquer fear and laziness and started acting! They could, I could, and you can too! The Universe loves and rewards those who work diligently! Act, and you will attract what you've been dreaming of and longing for a long time.

WHY ARE YOU HERE?

If you've been reading this chapter attentively, you've probably already realized your purpose in life and understood why you've come into this incarnation. The answer to this question is multifaceted. However, if you break it down into individual parts, everything will fall into place, and life will become more orderly, vibrant, and meaningful. So, why are you here?

"Your particle of Universal energy has come into this embodiment of a biological shell to live through your unique life experience; maximize positive energy growth through happiness and love; fulfill your purpose; develop measures to generate new knowledge, find solutions, and transform matter around you."

It might sound a bit convoluted, but there's nothing in this answer that you're not already familiar with. Let's take a little more time to explore each part of this concept to reinforce the new information and form a coherent picture.

"Your particle of Universal energy..." is your inner energy - your Soul. It's just a tiny piece of the General Universal Energy. This article is the foundation of your life.

"...has come into this embodiment of a biological shell to..." Every form of life has its biological shell, a particular material. For you, it's your human body. "Into this embodiment" because there have been and will be other material forms into which a part of your inner energy will transition. After the death of the current shell, your energy will move into the Family Tree. Later, it will transition into General Universal Energy and eventually into another material embodiment, continuing the cycle of Life in the Universe.

"Live through your unique life experience." You've been granted unique freedom of action in this embodiment. The Universe has breathed Life into your biological shell, but it can't control us like puppets. You have the right to decide how to spend your allotted time. How much to sleep, what to eat, whom to interact with, make friends, build a family, which decisions to make, where to travel, and what brings you happiness. Yes, your birthplace, time, and circumstances have left their mark on your life, but it's just a starting point. Set the right goals for yourself and act to achieve them.

"Maximize positive energy growth through happiness and love." Your emotions and actions will determine whether you nurture positive or negative aspects of your inner energy. Starting with a limited energy reserve, you should discover the unique material that brings you the most happiness. Through happiness and love for

kindred souls, you'll maximize your inner energy and, in turn, multiply the General Universal Energy. This is how Life evolves and thrives in the Universe.

"Fulfill your purpose." Finding and fulfilling the task assigned to you by the Universe takes work. Many go through life without ever understanding their purpose. For Life as a whole, it's not so critical. The Universe assigns similar tasks to different biological shells to achieve specific results. Millions of artists, poets, businesspeople, chefs, doctors, teachers, and so on exist. Each has a unique purpose, and so do you. Discover your talents, determine your soul's desires, listen to yourself and the hints from the Universe, find your purpose, make it your number one goal, and start acting. Remember that to achieve your goals, the Universe guides Life through hints, events, and the influence of all living beings on the matter around and each other. You are a part of this Universal design.

When my grandmother Tasya passed away, my father pondered, "Why do the best people always go first?" I found the answer to this question many years later. "Because the best people fulfill all their assigned tasks completely. They've fulfilled their purpose in life, developed their souls to the fullest, and are ready for a new reincarnation and destiny."

And finally, but no less critical: *"Develop the measure to use it to generate new knowledge, find solutions, and transform matter around you."* Your brain and intellect are crucial to understanding and interacting with the Universe. You also create and expand multiple measures by developing your mind through reading, gaining knowledge in various fields, and embracing the arts. With their help, you can gather information about the matter that makes up everything in the Universe. The more measures you have in your mind, the more effectively you interact with the Universe and the better you live your life.

When you accumulate sufficient measures and information, you will undoubtedly be visited by a Muse, or the Universe will reward you with a revelation. In these moments, you can create something new: inventions, discoveries, or works of art, and find new solutions to the tasks at hand. All of this will help transform the matter around you, change processes, and spawn new directions in the development of Life and humanity, in particular. This is how the Universe evolves, and Life undergoes evolution.

As you may have guessed, you are just a speck of life in the Universe, but a very important one! You are part of the grand design and the evolutionary path of Life in the Universe! You are like a cell in the human body - unique but a part of a very complex and large organism. You are the link between the material and energetic aspects of the Universe! We cannot evolve, develop, and move forward without life forms like us. Without Life, the Universe would freeze like a stone in the vast expanse of dark matter.

Life is that unique "Wonder in the Universe" that must be preserved and available to us! This Wonder exists within each of us! Within me and you. You are the "Wonder in the Universe"! You are Life itself! You are the Universe!

REVELATION AND ENLIGHTENMENT

“

"The Universe unveils new ideas only to a mind brimming with knowledge and open to exploration."

”

One could have concluded the book in the previous chapter. But I believe you already have questions: "Where did he acquire all these thoughts and knowledge? Why is he so confident in the authenticity of his conclusions? What inspired him to write this book? And what was the pivotal moment in his life that changed everything?"

These are entirely valid questions to ask of me. The answer is simple: "Throughout my life, I have accumulated a wealth of knowledge from various sources and gained diverse life experiences, upon which I based all these conclusions at the moment of revelation."

The Universe has often rewarded my curious mind with insights known as the 'Muse.' It has helped me generate new ideas. But once, I had an extraordinary experience I named 'revelation.' It granted me knowledge that forms the foundation of this book and divided my life into 'before' and 'after.' But all things in their time. Let us begin with the fundamental definition of revelations and enlightenment as I understand them.

Enlightenment (I prefer to call it the 'Muse') is a cognitive process wherein new ideas take shape within your brain based on previously acquired knowledge and experience. It is that moment when your creative side introduces something novel to the world, and you exclaim, "Eureka !"

The Muse can bestow ideas upon you in entirely different realms. You might paint a vivid picture, write a captivating book, compose a lyrical poem, create a brilliant collection of new clothing, devise a melodious tune that soothes the ear or conceive an engaging computer game idea. However, the Muse is not limited to creativity alone. You can find solutions to complex engineering problems, discover new chemical formulas, develop a remedy for an incurable illness, design an incredible architectural structure, and much more.

The Muse knows no bounds in its quest to enlighten you with new ideas. What matters to her is the knowledge you bring and the place you choose for your "rendezvous." With expertise, it's pretty simple. The Muse doesn't bring anything new with her. She won't hand you a ready-made formula, poem, or book. The Muse is responsible for the process of idea generation. To achieve this, she requires a solid foundation of knowledge and a diverse range of information she gathers through various means. The greater your knowledge base, the easier it will be for the Muse to generate new ideas, and the more vibrant and captivating the results will be.

As for the "place of seclusion," think of the Muse as a modest creature that shies away from revealing itself to the world and prefers to remain alone with you. The seclusion process with the Muse must be intimate, with no one else present. After all, she is easily frightened away. Finding a secluded spot where you can be alone with your thoughts and the Muse is essential. Choose a separate closed room, an office, or a quiet corner in a larger space. Try to assume the most comfortable and relaxed posture possible. Minimize distracting factors: turn off your phone and the internet, ask your loved ones not to disturb you, and remove any unnecessary items that might divert your attention.

And most importantly, strive to enter a "trance state." Immerse yourself completely in your thoughts. Turn off all extraneous sensory perceptions as if nothing exists around you except your inner voice. Close your eyes, breathe slowly and calmly, and relax your body. You must delve deep within yourself and reach a state akin to meditation. This will help you concentrate better on your thoughts and hear the Muse's whispers more distinctly. When the active thinking process begins, you will listen to the gentle voice of the Muse whispering a brilliant new idea. Her song will flow like magic. Please do not attempt to analyze, evaluate, or comprehend it. Just trust it and heed her wisdom.

I am well acquainted with the Muse. She visits me frequently. I was born with the gifts of a creator and a creative individual. Throughout my life, I've been seeking an outlet for my creative energy. Sometimes, I write poetry songs and invent various bedtime stories for my children. There was a period when I wrote screenplays for full-length movies and dreamt of conquering Hollywood. My profession as a programmer obliges me to create new software code, written like a narrative, steeped in logic. I came up with ideas for new computer games. And yes, now I am writing this book.

All these creative impulses have always been accompanied by the goddess of creation - my Muse. We share close and productive relationships. The Muse often visits me at night. I jokingly call this process "sleeping with the Muse." The perfect time and place for us is late at night and a soft bed. The absence of light and noise, closed eyes, and a relaxed body allow me to delve deep into my thoughts. Focusing on a single idea gives my mind the freedom to dance with the Muse and give birth to new ideas.

At this moment, the most crucial thing is not to interrupt this beautiful "dance of creation." Do not analyze or criticize the new information. Just allow the flow of thoughts to rush forward like a beam of light through the Universe. And record it ! Otherwise, most of the reviews will slip away by morning. For such occasions, I used to keep my "idea notebook" by the bed and write down all the new ideas that came to me at night.

I used that dark blue velvet-covered notebook for a long time. It still resides with me, holding a treasure trove of unrealized ideas. This notebook travels with me to new cities, countries, and continents. But in today's world of technology, I've switched to recording thoughts in an "electronic notebook," a standard app on my phone. The reasons for this are simple: the phone is always at hand, day and night; it doesn't require additional lighting, and I can record ideas in any position. I've even learned to type with two fingers faster than I can write by hand.

So, how does the process of communication with my Muse work? It's straightforward. At a specific moment of mental concentration, ideas begin to flow naturally. Sometimes, it's a small stream, and at other times, it's like Niagara Falls. Words arrange themselves into sentences, visual images emerge one after another, and ideas seem to appear out of nowhere. All I must do is keep my mind open and enjoy the creation process.

That's how I wrote poetry. Words seemed to materialize out of thin air, and I assembled them into rhyme. Similarly, I wrote movie scripts. The story, characters, conflicts, and three-act narrative structure appeared in my imagination as if I were watching a ready-made movie. It was as if I were sitting in a movie theatre with a notebook and pen, jotting down what was happening on the screen.

The same is happening now as I write this book. Words flow onto the paper like snowflakes gently falling to the ground, creating patterns of sentences, paragraphs, and chapters. I always savor this magnificent dance with the Muse. And when she next appears at your doorstep, remember to enjoy this unforgettable moment of creative impulse and the birth of something new! After all, this is part of your unique life and the evolution of the Universe! You are changing the Universe here and now! Savor this moment!

If enlightenment (the Muse) is a state of creative impulse and generating new ideas, what is "revelation" in my understanding? Revelation is a process like enlightenment, but its energetic charge is tens or even hundreds of times more potent. Enlightenment gives birth to a new idea and lasts for a short period, such as an hour or two. On the other hand, Revelation is like an endless stream of Muses lining up, extending far beyond the horizon. Communicating with these Muses stretches for long hours and sometimes days of continuous thought flow.

The main difference between revelation and enlightenment lies in the "scale" of the generated ideas. With the Muse, ideas typically stay within one knowledge area or question. For example, you might write a poem, devise a formula for a new chemical element, or design a rocket to the Moon. This requires knowledge and information in specific domains, facilitating the idea's inception.

With the revelation, it's a different story. It's like a powerful, energetic flow from the Universe enters your mind. Your brain starts working with astonishing efficiency. Any thoughts that enter this flow instantly trigger a cascade of new ideas. To access the necessary information for these ideas, the brain delves so deeply into its memory that it retrieves long-lost memories.

Physically, if you experience enlightenment, a meeting with the Muse, your biological shell will likely undergo a pleasant, relaxed state. Your mind will find serenity and ecstasy in the birth of new ideas.

The feelings you experience during revelation are akin to being run over by the "bulldozer of Universal Energy." The thought stream is so immense that it feels like your brain is on the brink of boiling and exploding from an information overload. This leads to sleepless nights, finger calluses from constant note-taking, and unimaginable emotional fluctuations linked to reliving long-forgotten memories.

I believe that many people on Earth enjoy pleasant evenings with their Muse, but only a few experience revelations. In religious terms, revelation is "direct conversation with God through the soul." It's a complex emotional and physical state, but the result is worth it!

From the perspective of our brain's functioning, meeting the Muse and receiving revelations are states where the brain reaches a new level of productivity compared to ordinary thinking. The exchange of electrical impulses between neurons intensifies with each new thought. Imagination, creative and rational thinking, creativity, and memory all come into play. The only difference is that the Muse activates a slightly more significant portion of the brain than ordinary daily thoughts, while revelations involve a substantial part of our consciousness.

Birthing a new idea during the Enlightenment is akin to playing with building blocks. Colorful cubes of various sizes representing our accumulated knowledge in different areas are scattered on the floor before the Muse. The Muse's task is to construct a magical castle from these cubes, to be later inhabited by princesses, unicorns, and dragons. Initially, the Muse selects cubes of the right size and color. Then, she starts stacking them on top of each other, exploring combinations to achieve the desired outcome. If there's enough material, the Muse will create a magnificent masterpiece. However, if she lacks the necessary blocks, the castle will crumble in her hands, never becoming a part of the architectural landscape of thought.

The process of revelation can be compared to sieving for grains of truth amid a sea of knowledge. Imagine that a bag of knowledge, information, memories, and experiences has been emptied. You'll need to sift through everything irrelevant to extract the grain of truth. Sieving is a process opposite to typical sifting. Instead of grains falling from the top to the bottom, they rise from the bottom upwards. An invisible force whips them up in a vortex toward the sky. With each new whirlwind turn, grains closer to the truth rise higher and higher. But some grains remain at the bottom. Only those closest to the truth ascend. With each new vortex, we discard the unnecessary, and fewer and fewer grains remain. Until you hold in your hand just one "Grain of Truth." That's the one for which the Universe bestowed that unforgettable revelation upon you. This truth is the meaning of your life, your "Holy Grail," and your "Divine Gift." This grain of truth became the realization of my life's purpose.

I depicted the process of revelation on the cover of this book but in the form of the Universe. It's as if, in the whirlwind of truth-seeking, the stars of the Universe are spinning, and something greater than us, beyond comprehension, finds that "Grain of Truth." This image came to me during my moment of revelation. In that pivotal moment, I received only a tiny fragment of ideas and knowledge from the Universe. My experience of revelation gave birth to the idea of writing this book. Turn the page, and you'll learn what my revelation was like.

MY REVELATION EXPERIENCE

"

"Sleepless nights, physical exhaustion, and mental fatigue are worth the revelation received from the Universe."

"

This chapter proved to be the most emotionally challenging for me during the writing process. Nevertheless, it is no less important than the others. On the one hand, I want to provide you with a complete view of the entire picture and describe everything that happened to me, as these events formed the foundation of this book. On the other hand, my truth may resonate with your perception of the world. I'm apprehensive about openly sharing my memories and thoughts, baring my soul before you. I hope it's worth it. The decision is yours.

My revelation experience began in the city of Gdansk, Poland, on one of the November days in 2021. At that time, my family and

I had been living in Poland for just over eight months. I had spent the previous 37 years of my life in Ukraine. However, complex circumstances, the war in the East, and a lack of stability, reliability, and faith in the future compelled me to move to another country. After receiving a job offer from Poland and consulting with my family, we decided to give this wonderful country, which is spiritually close to Ukrainians, a chance.

In the autumn of 2021, COVID-19 was still rampant. We tried to stay home as much as possible and minimize contact with people. There was little need to visit public places. I worked from home. Occasionally, we went to the park and the sea for walks with the children and went to the store for groceries. On November 6, 2021, we went to the hair salon to freshen up my wife, Hanna and our son Lev. Nothing foreshadowed trouble. However, all indirect evidence suggests that on that day, we caught COVID-19. Perhaps the hair salon contributed to this, or Yeva's school sent their "regards" the day before. We skillfully avoided the virus throughout 2020 in Ukraine and almost a year in Poland. But the time had come, and there was no chance to avoid encountering it anymore.

Initially, Hanna felt unwell, followed by our daughter, and I started feeling ill. The girls lost their sense of taste and smell. Their bodies were worn out from illness and fatigue. All signs pointed to one thing: it was COVID-19. On November 16, the three of us took COVID-19 tests. The little children were not subjected to the test, so Lev escaped the swabbing procedure. It could have been a more pleasant procedure, but it was necessary. On the 17th, we received positive results and knew we had COVID-19.

For the next ten days, our bodies fought the virus on their own. The illness progressed in a very unusual way. My body experienced sensations I had never felt before. The virus seemed to scan it for vulnerabilities from head to toe. A pounding headache gradually spread throughout my body. My neck ached, and I couldn't lift my arms. Then everything seemed to contract inside. My back hurt like I had been carrying sandbags for a week. Then, it was the turn of my legs. The virus left nothing untouched. Everything that had ever ached in my life was throbbing in pinpoint pain. My previously operated right knee, sore lower back, and stomach—even the vaccination mark on my shoulder had its say. The insidious virus and the strange sensations associated with it were not something I would want to experience again.

I felt severe malaise and a fever on the third or fourth day. By then, food had already lost its taste, and the world had lost all its scents. I took fever-reducing pills for several days. However, they only provided temporary relief, and a few hours later, I was burning with fever again. It got worse. Since the beginning of the COVID-19 pandemic in 2020, we have purchased a small pulse oximeter to monitor blood oxygen saturation, which should generally be 98-99% for a healthy person. My saturation levels started to drop. The device showed 94-95%. I began to experience mild shortness of breath and difficulty breathing. It was clear that there were issues with my lungs.

I consulted a doctor over the phone, and she advised me to go to the hospital for an examination and blood test. Moreover, the ten-day quarantine ended, and I might no longer be contagious. I drove to the hospital on the same day in my car. Fortunately, Gdansk was a small city, and it took only fifteen minutes. Driving was quite an experience when your hands felt like cotton, your head was pounding, and your body was on fire. The destination was the "Pomeranian Center for Infectious Diseases and Tuberculosis" in Gdansk. Before they called me in for the examination, I had to breathe some fresh air at the entrance to the reception area while they were attending to a patient who had arrived in an ambulance.

The examination took several hours, a standard procedure for such situations—blood tests, lung auscultation, and oxygen saturation measurement—96%. Waiting in the fresh air had worked in my favor. The attending physician informed me that the situation was not critical, but there were signs of lung function deterioration. She offered two options. The first was to take a medical certificate and go home to self-treat. The second was to stay and be hospitalized under the supervision of doctors for a few days. Considering it was a city infectious disease department; my imagination painted a less-than-pleasant picture of the local wards. I immediately wanted to go home to avoid catching anything else. I took the medical certificate and hastily left the department, as it turned out, not for long.

That night, around 3 o'clock, I woke up gasping for air, oxygen deprivation setting in. I put a pulse oximeter on my finger. My pulse raced on the screen, the device beeped, and it displayed a saturation of 92%. My saturation had dropped, and breathing had become even more difficult. Five minutes later, the thermometer showed 38.5 degrees Celsius. At that moment, Hanna and I realized we couldn't delay any longer and had to return to the hospital.

I dialed 911 and called for an ambulance. The ambulance arrived in about ten to fifteen minutes. At that time, I gathered the necessary items for my stay in the hospital and took the medical certificate I had received earlier in the day. Sitting on the edge of the bed, I couldn't take my eyes off the pulse oximeter—90%. Breathing became even more complicated, my heart pounded, and my brain contemplated the following stages of events. The prospects didn't look promising.

Upon the arrival of the ambulance, the doctor examined me, listened to my lungs, took down my medical history, and checked my saturation using a more professional pulse oximeter—86%. It was unanimous; I needed to be admitted to the hospital. I hugged Hanna tightly and got into the ambulance. The trip was short but exhausting. My head was spinning, and I was burning up. They placed an oxygen mask on me since I found breathing increasingly difficult. A severe coughing fit began when the ambulance stopped at the reception area, where I had been the day before. It was then that I coughed up blood for the first time. My "adventures" and the fight for my life began on November 25, 2021, in Room 108 of the infectious disease department in Gdansk.

The first ten days were the toughest. An X-ray showed that my lungs were 40% affected. Breathing was a struggle, and I was hooked up to an oxygen machine. My temperature regularly spiked, and they tried to lower it with fever-reducing medications, but it only worked briefly. My condition deteriorated. At some point, I began coughing up blood more and more. The virus was wreaking havoc in my lungs. I would fill a small plastic dish with blood each day.

Panic and anxiety grew within me and among the people close to me. I received two IV drips each morning and evening. They served me a small bucket of various pills. In the morning, I received injections in my stomach to thin my blood. I became inseparable from the oxygen mask for the following 18 days. Even going to the bathroom without it felt like conquering Mount Everest.

I felt worse than I had ever felt in my life. I had been coughing up blood for several days. My temperature constantly rose to 39 degrees Celsius. My body ached and throbbed with pain. I was losing hope and the will to live. One day, for some reason, the nurses began giving me double doses of medication in my stomach in the morning and evening. This alarmed me. My condition worsened significantly. The doctors' only hope lay in an unapproved experimental COVID-19 treatment and the strength and determination of my body to fight the virus. I signed consent to receive the experimental drug, and my treating doctor administered the first of five doses. All that was left was to hope for a miracle.

In the evening, when despair overwhelmed me, I called home. Hearing how my beloved Hanna barely held back tears, and our daughter cried in the background, I realized that everyone was losing hope and fearing the worst outcome. Hanna tried to encourage me, instilling hope to keep fighting for my life. But negative thoughts kept creeping into my mind uninvited. In response, I whispered how much I loved them, wished them "sweet dreams," and hung up the phone. I had no strength to fight; I collapsed on the bed and closed my eyes. All that remained for me was to pray.

I turned to the Universe, to God, with a plea for help in this challenging moment. Then I remembered my parents. My beloved mother and father passed away in 2020, and I missed them dearly during these difficult days: my mother's smile and my father's jokes.

Mentally, conjuring the images of my parents was not difficult. I embraced them with all my strength. I told them how much I loved them and missed them. I asked for their help in battling this insidious illness. "It's too early for me to join you now. I can't leave my beloved ones alone—Hanna and our children. I implore you, if it's within your power, help me get through these difficult days, recover, and return home alive to my family." My plea for help was a mixture of desperation and hope. It was all I could do at that moment. With these thoughts, I descended into the realm of dreams.

By morning, I had a strange and unusual vision. It may have been a dream or my imagination. A funnel opened above me, extending into the heavens. It seemed to beckon me. Its semi-transparent grayish walls felt so real. Inside the horn, I saw white and blue silhouettes of my mother and father, as if they were energy clouds. My mother stood on the left and my father on the right. Behind them were silhouettes resembling my grandmothers, although I wasn't entirely sure. The images of my parents radiated hope and love. They reached out to me. I reached for them and hugged them like I hadn't embraced them in a thousand years. They didn't say a word, but at that moment, I felt a sense of relief and the certainty that everything would be all right.

Upon waking, I called my beloved wife, Hanna, and told her about my vision. Her response surprised me: "It sounds like the Family Tree." Hanna had heard and read about it somewhere before. That was the first time I learned of a "Family Tree." Hanna explained that it represents our deceased ancestors, with women on the left and men on the right. She said that within the Family Tree lies a connection to our lineage and its strength. This was my first connection to the Family Channel, where I saw my Family Tree—this moment marked the beginning of my revelation.

This was a turning point. It was my parents who helped me find the strength to fight the illness. In the following days, my body began to recover gradually. The fever finally stopped heating me, and my temperature dropped. The presence of blood during coughing became less and altogether ceased after a couple of days. A pleasant growling returned to my stomach. Having an appetite was always a sign that I was getting better. The number of injections to thin the blood was reduced, and the blueish tint on my belly slowly started to regain its standard color. They also began to reduce the oxygen supply. Breathing on my own without the mask was still challenging, but I could finally eat without the breathlessness of a marathon runner, like in the first days at the hospital. And I finally got some rest. During these days, I slept half a day and didn't leave.

The care of my loved ones significantly contributed to my recovery. Love and support from family can work wonders, just as much as pills, IVs, and injections. I also started taking a high dose of vitamins. Hanna found a good vitaminization scheme for this virial infection and bought everything necessary. Friends didn't stay behind either. Regular calls and messages asking, "How are you feeling?" lifted my spirits and instilled faith in a speedy recovery. My childhood friend, Pasha, occasionally brought me care packages from home with big bags filled with "fruit vitamins." It turned out to be so wonderful to have a big family and a bunch of friends all around the world!

My daughter, Yeva, gave me a small family photo measuring five by 5 centimeters. In it, we were all smiling and happy. We took this photo in one of those street photo booths. The booth was designed for only two people. It was fun to squeeze all four of us in and fit four heads into a small photo. But the picture turned out so lively. It seemed to radiate laughter and joy from that happy moment.

Hanna and Yeva wrote on the back of the photo, "We love you (3 hearts). We're waiting and missing you. We miss you very much (heart). Get well soon!!! (big heart)." This photo wouldn't let me give up in the fight for my life. It evoked the warmest and happiest memories and warmed my heart with the love of my dear ones. Yeva often made me such "talismans." When I went on business trips, she would sneakily place them in my belongings. It was enjoyable to discover them randomly. These talismans supported me in difficult moments of parting. Thank you, my daughter, for them (three big red hearts and a kiss) !

I thank all of you: family, friends, guardian angels, my parents, grandmothers, and my lineage ! Thank you, Universe ! It's thanks to all of you that I am here now ! Alive, healthy, and safe. I write these lines.

The long days of recovery were incredibly productive. I read a lot on various topics. I studied the history of humanity, from World War I to current events. I analyzed why relations between Ukraine and its neighbors had become so heated. I also read about international organizations, the banking system, economic crises, securities markets, and stock exchanges. I analyzed significant issues humanity faces: catastrophes, epidemics, hunger, lack of clean drinking water, overpopulation in some countries, uneven distribution of resources, and excessive consumption.

I returned to my old research on where raising our children might be relatively safe without the constant pressure of circumstances and state politics. About ten years ago, the idea of migration first crossed my mind. At that time, Canada seemed like the most suitable option. But it was almost impossible back then due to the complex immigration program.

This time, the decision was finally made. All paths led me back to the land of the maple leaf. A deep, additional analysis of economic indicators, geographic data, government policies, and immigration opportunities in Canada convinced me of the correctness of the chosen direction. It was the first time I realized that Canada is the "Noah's Ark of Humanity." It's a self-sufficient country, almost detached from all other nations, filled with many different resources, and it has the second-largest territory in the world. It's home to the most diverse races and ethnicities. It's as if in Noah's Ark, there's "a pair for every person." A firm and final decision was made to migrate to Canada.

I analyzed many different information and contemplated during those days. My brain started to rev up. It became easier to understand, memorize, and see the big picture of the world. Thoughts constantly swirled in my head. My brain seemed to absorb new knowledge like a sponge. It was as if it was preparing for something important.

Revelation and a flood of creative thoughts began gradually and gained momentum. At first, the Muse visited me. She directed the flow of thoughts towards my forgotten idea - to create a new fantastic world with a captivating story about a fallen angel. This idea first came to me about ten years ago. I jotted down story sketches in my notebook, described a couple of key characters, and set these notes aside for better times.

Shortly after that, the idea of writing a screenplay for a feature film based on this fallen angel concept came to me. At that time, I was studying the art of screenwriting and working on several projects simultaneously. The main idea remained a mere sketch in my "Idea notebook," but it catalyzed another story. This is where the Muse and I got to work. After months of painstaking effort, the "Diabolically Divine" screenplay was ready. Unfortunately, it seemed that this film was not destined to see the light of day. I sent the script to several film studios but received nothing but disinterest from the film industry. At that moment, I realized that writing screenplays for movies wouldn't bring me closer to my dream of creating something meaningful. So, I began searching for a new way to express my creative energy. Perhaps someday, I will return to the screenplay "Diabolically Divine," rethink it, polish it, and still see it come to life on screen. Only time will tell.

During my last three days in the hospital, when the flow of creative ideas rushed into my consciousness like a tsunami, I worked obsessively on the concept of a computer game based on the old story from my notebook about the fallen Angel. My mind was so open to the Universe that the flow of creative ideas never ceased. I could only tap my fingers on the smartphone screen, jotting down notes. I was so engrossed in the process that I forgot to eat and slept only three to four hours daily.

It was the most productive time of my life! I recorded all the ideas that came to mind, spending about forty hours on notes in three days. Ignoring typos and errors, my fingers danced in a whimsical pattern of words on the screen. There was one thought in my head: "Don't miss anything important." I was afraid that the flow of thoughts and ideas would suddenly end. But fatigue overwhelmed me. My hands shook. My fingers stumbled on the keyboard. The callus on my pinky, which supported the phone, throbbed with pain. The image in front of my eyes blurred, and I couldn't focus. My eyes felt as dry as the Sahara Desert. I had to blink and concentrate on the screen constantly. But I continued taking notes as if my fingers were dancing to the melody of the Universe.

Simultaneously, I kept a small diary to preserve my insights and new ideas. Alongside creative ideas, the next phase of revelation brought forth memories of my life and knowledge gathered from various books and life experiences.

Memories emerged from so long ago that I had never recalled these events. It was as if my memory had come to life and started working with renewed vigor. This revelation was for someone who only sometimes remembers what happened yesterday! Images and details were so vivid as if I had repeatedly travelled back and relived these events.

Memories of my carefree childhood resurfaced memories of all the elementary schools I attended, friends in the neighborhood, and memories of my beloved grandmothers. Then came the years of high school in the senior classes, college, marriage, the birth of children, and numerous relocations in search of a better life. It was as if my entire life flashed before my eyes.

While my thoughts travelled through my memories, I began to piece together fragments of various information acquired from life lessons, circumstances, and books I had read over the past 30 years. Fascinating nuances and details came to the surface. All this started forming into one big picture from a thousand puzzle pieces. I didn't fully grasp what that picture was yet, but I began to sense notes of importance in the unfolding events.

I received answers to questions and new knowledge, one after the other. It was unique and priceless! I acquired vast information as a springboard to generate numerous new ideas. At a certain point in my contemplation, I pondered, "Why did I fall ill and end up in the hospital precisely now? Is there a purpose or a logical explanation behind this?" So, I asked the Universe, "Why was I sent to the trial of battling COVID-19?" As it turned out later, it was the right question to ask! The ability to pose the right questions means receiving the necessary answers. Sending the question to the Universe, I once again immersed myself in the fabricated world of the fallen Angel for a future game. It was as if the Muse didn't want to part with me.

I outlined the main storyline, key characters, core mechanics, progressions, and gameplay for the game. I crafted a game world complete with a map, all the biomes (gaming zones), and the main structures within them. I described several key cutscenes, devised various quests, enemy types, and bosses, and created different weapon types. All of this, I wove into an exhilarating game. I could see everything happening as if I had already played it, conquering a new, captivating universe.

Over the past few years, I revisited the idea of creating this game only a few times. The planning was far from what I had described during my illness days in the hospital. I understood that creating an AAA-level gaming project alone was simply impossible. These are top-tier games with massive budgets and teams of hundreds of specialists. Therefore, I always postponed this idea for later.

But then, in just a few days, I conceptualized and described a vast and vibrant virtual world. People in the gaming industry will understand what I'm talking about. Just take my word for it: I put in immense work! It delighted me immensely, but it also made me cautious. Never in my life had I communicated so long and productively with the Muse, even though I had encountered her a hundred times before.

I brought together the entire world of my fabricated gaming universe and breathed a sigh of relief. Returning to the real world, I regained my composure, attended to everyday matters, and got some rest. When I woke up, I spoke with my family. I had missed them so much! The separation had been unbearably harsh. But thanks to the internet and mobile connectivity, I could see my family and converse with my loved ones.

On that day, I noticed another strange thing. The skin on my hands seemed to have aged like an older adult. It was tough, wrinkled, and dry. This concerned me. I had seen hands like these before, but they belonged to my father, who was 63 years old, not to me at 37. Another strange phrase came to mind: "holding God's hand." I am trying to remember precisely where I heard it, but the description seemed fitting. After enduring complex events or illnesses, some people exhibited aged hand skin, as if they had "held God's hand," and He had granted them the strength to recover. My skeptical mind and critical thinking immediately found an explanation for the aged hands – prolonged oxygen deprivation to the body. Later, I started regularly applying cream to my hands, which Hanna had given me, and my skin gradually returned to normal. We will never know whether I touched the Universe or if it was just my imagination in the absence of oxygen.

On December 12, 2021, my oxygen saturation normalized – 96-97%. Fantastic! I measured it every hour throughout the day and dubbed this statistic "my ticket home." I spent half of the previous day without an oxygen mask. And on December 12, I bid farewell to it entirely, disconnecting the oxygen supply device.

It was my mother Raya's birthday. She's Hanna's mom. This incredible, kind, caring, and wise woman had long become my second mother. She's one of the best women I've ever met. So, during her birthday celebration, I wanted to make her happy by showing my face without an oxygen mask.

In those days, Raya and Sergey, Hanna's parents, were also battling COVID-19. We were separated by 2392 kilometers, but our struggle against the virus united us. I was deeply concerned about them. With my fighting attitude, I wanted to show them I was doing well and boost their spirits. My father had passed away from this dreadful virus, which had also nearly taken me to the other side. I understood how challenging it was for our parents' bodies to cope with COVID-19 and how imperfect, sometimes helpless, medicine could be. Thanks to the Universe, everything worked out! The parents handled it better than I did. I am grateful to you, Universe, for this!

A significant sign of recovery was the return of my sense of humor. On that day, I started joking again. I hadn't even realized that I hadn't joked for 18 days! Those who know me, my brother, my sister, and my father are familiar with our "family sense of humor and wit." Humor is in our blood.

My father was always the center of attention at any gathering and the life of the party among friends. He made everyone around him burst into laughter. My friends were always curious about how I became so witty and where I knew hundreds of jokes from. That was until they met my father. Once, my brother Sergey told jokes for four hours when we visited relatives in Crimea. Some of my family members live there: uncles, aunts, cousins, and half-siblings on my father's side.

Once at work, they tried to test my knowledge of jokes, led by the Scrum Master. I told him that I knew jokes for almost any life situation. He devised different topics for several weeks and tried to expose me. He failed, but everyone had a good laugh.

So, when I cracked a few jokes with myself and on the phone with loved ones in the hospital, I realized that I hadn't joked for all those days. It made me wary, and then it delighted me. After all, it was a clear sign that I was recovering and returning to my old life. As you probably remember, my father left us when his sense of humor deserted him. I believe humor was his life energy, just like mine.

On the morning of December 12th, as I was thinking about my parents and grandparents, ancient memories flooded in with such intensity that it felt like I was reliving them. I wept uncontrollably, unable to contain the tears of the bitter loss of loved ones. I relived the tragedy of their deaths once again. My heart was pounding out of my chest, my hands were shaking, and my nerves were shaken to the core. I knew the doctor would come for the morning check-up soon, and being in such a state wouldn't help me get discharged from the hospital any faster. But I couldn't control my emotions.

Later, I called Hanna and pondered, "Did these dates coincidentally align?" My beloved tracked down the coincidences and recognized the significance of specific dates. On November 6, 2021, Hanna, Lev, and I were at the hair salon. Presumably, that's where we caught COVID-19. It was my father's birthday. Nine days later, the first symptoms of the illness appeared, and I started feeling unwell. It was November 15, 2021, the day my father passed away.

The path to solitude on a hospital bed for revelation was a "gift from my father."

My mother also "participated" in these events. Hanna noticed that our foreign passports had received "Polish red stamps" on April 11, 2021. This was official confirmation that we could legally live, work, and study in Poland and would soon receive "Residence Cards." These cards are equivalent to the "Permanent Resident Card" in Canada and the "Green Card" in the United States. The red stamps signified successful legalization and the beginning of a new life in Poland. This date was my mother's birthday. It was destined for me to be in Gdansk during this period of my life, battle illness, and go through this revelation experience. Thank you, Mom and Dad, for your "generous gifts" !

Then Hanna and I remembered that, from an astrological perspective, I had a challenging period. We fell ill during the "eclipse corridor." For me, it was a not-so-simple "karma period." At that time, my beloved told me that we receive what is fated for us in the eclipse corridor, and we have no choice but to accept it. What I experienced during those days of illness was karma preordained for me, a consequence of the lives I had lived before...

I know how some people regard astrology, and I am not able to persuade or condemn them. Everyone believes in what they want. Hanna had been fascinated by astrology since childhood. In her adult life, this interest was rekindled with renewed vigor. I had always been a skeptic. My knowledge of astrology was limited to memories of my mother reading weekly horoscopes in a magazine and sincerely believing in them. At the time, it all seemed like mere fantasy to me.

However, in recent years, Hanna and I delved into the study of astrology—my beloved even completed relevant courses. We tested astrology on ourselves to see if it worked. I can confidently say that astrology works. Perhaps not at 100% or not exactly as you might expect, but it does work. At least for us, it has worked in many situations and helped us make numerous correct decisions. Most importantly, like a missing puzzle piece, astrology has explained the processes and changes around us. When people couldn't understand why difficult times had come, astrology provided us with the answers crucial for understanding the chaos in the world. They were particularly relevant during 2020 and subsequent years, from COVID-19 to the war in Ukraine in 2022.

Some may call astrology pseudoscience or nonsense, while others may chuckle. But astrology is merely another measure people use to explain the processes occurring in the Universe. Astrology is not as perfect as mathematics or physics, but it works. It has helped me and my loved ones in many situations. So why not use another tool to make life easier and gain insight? Well, or at least "lay some straw if you understand when and where you might fall."

All these thoughts and memories swirled in my head throughout the day. I sat on the edge of the bed to stretch my back muscles a bit. Suddenly, everything around me seemed to freeze. It was as if I was plunging into emptiness. At that moment, the Universe provided me with an answer to the question, "Why was I sent the trial for battling COVID-19?" I understood that "I needed to be completely isolated from the world to realize my life's purpose. To understand how the Universe interacts with us. To know our place within it. To convey these thoughts to as many people as possible." Yes, yes. This was the answer to the very question people ask themselves throughout their lives, and not everyone finds a reply to: "Why was I born into this world? What is my purpose?"

I received the answer and saw my entire 37 years of life as if laid out in the palm of my hand. I connected all my life's events and critical moments into one path, the endpoint of which was my revelation. It was as if my entire life had led me to this moment. As if I had sifted out the truth from hundreds of grains. At that moment, I hadn't received all the knowledge and hadn't realized many things yet. But I was absolutely sure that my stay in the hospital was a necessity for my solitude and for gaining this revelation.

I became scared when I realized why the Universe had allowed me to experience those challenging days of battling COVID-19 and understood my purpose. My first thought was, "I hope Hanna believes me and doesn't think I've gone crazy! I'm talking to the Universe and my Family Tree, and they're responding to me! Isn't that borderline madness?" I panicked. The burden of responsibility placed on me by the Universe frightened me. But I was grateful to it for the answer and the priceless experience of those days of revelation.

I had plenty of new thoughts and ideas on that day. I worked on my game and contemplated my place and role in the Universe. Every hour, I measured my oxygen saturation. My desire to return home was powerful. As I lay down to sleep, I imagined my parents again, embracing them and thanking them for their gifts and this invaluable experience. I asked the Universe to "send me home tomorrow" and fell asleep.

I was discharged from the hospital the next day, on Monday, December 13th. My attending physician said that my condition had significantly improved, and my oxygen saturation was stable without needing an oxygen mask so that I could be discharged. However, she was concerned about the results of the D-dimer blood test.

I was confident that the doctor would send me home. Where did this confidence come from? It was also part of the Universe's answer: "I will stay in the hospital for as long as it takes to understand everything, accept it, and start a new path."

After a thorough examination and reviewing my test results and saturation measurements that I had kept for a couple of days without an oxygen mask, the doctor discharged me. She gave me a medical certificate for a whole month of recovery at home. There was only one condition: administering the blood-thinning injections in my abdomen and showing the D-Dimer blood test results to the local doctor. The paperwork and discharge process took a little while. That evening, I left my room number 108 in high spirits and full of hope.

I spent 19 days in the hospital without seeing my family. It was the most extended separation in our 16 years of marriage. Wandering through the hospital's dark corridors, searching for the exit, my legs seemed to carry me home alone. Stepping outside, a refreshing chill greeted me, and the abundance of oxygen rushed into my nostrils. My head started to spin. My body had not received such a massive dose of natural oxygen in 19 days. I barely reached a bench at the checkpoint and sat down to rest. While enjoying the frosty winter evening in Gdansk, I called a taxi.

I hoped the revelation had passed and I could finally rest. But I was wrong. Ideas flooded my brain once again. This time, they were the beginnings of the "Laws of the Universe." I had turned into a writing machine again. Words seemed to flow through my fingers. I didn't even realize how I got into the taxi, gave the address, and the car started moving. The driver tried to engage in conversation. He was a fellow countryman eager to chat, but I apologized and asked him not to distract me. My fingers typed away throughout the journey. I continued to write until the very last moment when the car stopped at my doorstep. I paid the driver and stumbled home.

My eyes were shining with happiness. "I'm home" echoed in my head every second. I rejoiced in everything around me like a little child: the familiar entrance, the Christmas tree in the hall, the elevator, our ninth floor, and the door to our apartment with the number 77.

I rang the doorbell. Goldy, our Miniature Yorkshire Terrier, barked. "I haven't heard her bark in so long!" I thought. A moment later, joyful cries of "Hooray! Dad's back!" came from behind the door. Tears welled up in my eyes. Hanna opened the door. I took a few steps forward. The bags fell to the floor from the weight. I took off my coat and collapsed on the floor behind them. I didn't have the strength to go any further; my heart was pounding out of my chest, and emotions overwhelmed me. The children and Hanna swarmed around me, holding me tighter and tighter in their arms. Goldie licked my hands and face with all her might. I paused for a moment to savor this moment of universal happiness. And I cried like a little child. "I'm alive. I'm home."

During those 19 days in the hospital, I tested my mind, brain, and biological shell. During the illness and stress, I had lost 10 kilograms. Fatigue, exhaustion, and muscle weakness prevented me from standing up straight. Looking in the mirror, it seemed I had aged ten years. I saw an unshaven, hunched, thin older man in the reflection. Such profound physical depletion was caused by the illness and the experiences I went through.

Upon returning home, the revelation didn't end; it even intensified. The flow of information continued for several more days. On the first evening, Hanna and I discussed the insights I had received. I was spewing thoughts and ideas at the speed of sound. There were so many of them. Everything I thought about that came to my mind was discussed. I'm grateful to Hanna for her support, understanding, and development of ideas. And for not handing me over to the "people in white coats." It was a wonderful and highly productive evening. I lay on the couch, exhausted but surrounded by children and the dog, and I was in seventh heaven. Thanks to my knowledge, the picture of our place in the Universe began to come together like a unified puzzle.

Creative thoughts and the understanding of the Laws of the Universe continued to wander between the neurons of my brain. The image of a funnel, filtering grains of knowledge for the sake of truth, came about during one of our discussions with Hanna. It appeared on its own. The image well represented the essence of my theory. And I immediately shared it with my beloved. My memory recorded the idea, and we continued our discussion. It was a genuinely productive and astonishing time!

How do I know that Universal Energy exists within us? It may sound wild, absurd, and bordering on madness, but I saw it. On that day, my brain activity was off the charts. Hanna and I constantly discussed new ideas and searched for confirmation in real life and other theories describing the Universe.

At some point, Hanna went to talk to Yeva, our daughter. They stood in the hallway, discussing something. I briefly lost myself in my thoughts. When I looked at my girls again, I couldn't believe my eyes. I saw their souls, but not as we usually imagine them. It was as if I saw their energetic system. It resembled a human nervous system with branches all over their bodies. Everything emitted a bluish-white light. I saw how a particle of Universal Energy circulated inside the biological shells of my girls.

Of course, like you, I thought it was madness. Or perhaps my imagination had run wild. Maybe it was hallucinations caused by the injections in my abdomen? Or was it exhaustion and lack of sleep? I briefly closed my eyes and tried to shake off these thoughts. When I looked at my girls again, I no longer saw anything that could raise concerns about my mental health. I breathed a sigh of relief, and Hanna and I continued brainstorming. I didn't bring up what I had seen and didn't dwell on it. Another thought flashed: "I hope they don't send me to the madhouse to a room with Napoleone." I already had an excess of information that defied logical explanation at first glance. And now the souls of my loved ones. "No, I'm not ready for this!"

My body was severely depleted from constant discussions, emotional outbursts, and lack of sleep. At some point, I felt an emptiness, as if I were an empty vessel with nothing but walls inside. The time it seemed to stop and lose its meaning. My biological shell and its existence were no longer as necessary in the face of realizing the truth about the Universe. It was as if there was something greater than me, more significant than our earthly problems, more excellent than everything surrounding us. Only the absolute truth was revealed: "The Meaning of Life in the Universe."

For a moment, I pondered death. Throughout my life, the unknown of what would happen after the death of my biological shell had frightened me. The skeptical part of my brain could not come up with an explanation. "Will the light just go out? Will I feel nothing? Will I even exist? Will I be able to know what my family will feel? Will I ever see them again?" All this terrified me—all this uncertainty.

But everything fell into place when I realized the soul would go to the Family Tree after death, close to loved ones. I understood that if my loved ones remembered me, I wouldn't lose my connection with them. I stopped fearing it When I realized there was life after death. This doesn't mean I no longer value or love my life. On the contrary! Today, the significance of my body and life is my number one priority. The longer my biological shell lasts, the longer I can be with my loved ones, the more goals I can achieve, and the more wisdom and experience I can accumulate and pass on to my children. I love my life! Thank you, parents, and thank you, Universe, for this priceless gift!

A few hours later, when my strength was nearly depleted, and our discussions ended, I collapsed on the couch like a bag of bones. Yet, I felt harmony, satisfaction, and happiness. To quiet the rushing stream of thoughts and get some rest, I buried my face in the pillow to create maximum darkness. My eyes were tightly closed, creating a pitch-black environment.

What I saw again stunned me. It was a white cloud with millions of bluish neurons and energetic charges racing between them. In complete darkness, I saw the front part of my brain working actively. Yes, it sounds strange and wild. But not as frightening as what I had seen in the energies of my girls. I observed how a part of my brain operated within my cranial cavity for a few seconds. The spectacle was so incredible that I couldn't tear my gaze away. Millions of neurons exchange energy, giving rise to thoughts. The white-blueish glow resembled a hologram of the brain. I thought,

"My brain is like the Universe, still so poorly understood by us and concealing many secrets."

And then, the skeptic in me returned, and I became scared. The thought raced through my mind: "Am I seeing my brain? This is complete nonsense!" I even shuddered. I jumped up, opening my eyes. It was not a dream, as only a few seconds had passed. But what I had witnessed deeply astounded me. I told Hanna about it. She made a few modest comments. And I jokingly changed the subject, not wanting to focus on what I had seen. We had already received much new information that day, more than enough. It was necessary to comprehend and digest what could be somehow logically explained.

Unfortunately, or perhaps fortunately, I never saw anything like that again. Neither particles of Universal Energy in my loved ones nor the workings of my brain. I chalked it up to exhaustion, overly active brain activity, the injections, emotional instability—anything to convince myself that I hadn't gone crazy. Otherwise, it would have been challenging to persuade other people that it wasn't a figment of my imagination.

A surge of brain activity on that day was very intense. I couldn't sleep at night, contemplating the information I had received and the transformations happening. Around 4 a.m., I had a revelation! I understood how everything was structured in the Universe! I rushed to the kitchen, grabbed a piece of paper, and, with trembling hands, drew the "Structure of the Universe" that you saw at the beginning of this book.

Yes, this picture became the foundation of this book and my current worldview. It was my revelation's sought-after "kernel of truth" describing our place in the Universe! This torn piece of paper with scribbles on it changed my perspective and life for the better! I hope it will change yours too.

At that moment, everything lost its meaning except for this truth. Sitting in silence and gazing at the diagram, I contemplated its plausibility. I pondered various hypotheses and real-life examples, trying to understand how they were interconnected with this diagram. After half an hour, my attempts to find flaws failed.

My heart danced in my chest again, emotions overflowed, and my soul trembled. My body and mind experienced "euphoria" – a powerful, sudden surge of happiness. I felt like I was glowing. I understood how to become happy and live an incredible life! My soul had never experienced such a strong emotion before. I thank the Universe for that moment! It was exquisite and magnificent!

After that, my stream of revelation ceased. I found the kernel I was searching for. Finally, after a long time, I could sleep well and rest. The rhythm of life gradually normalized. I contemplated writing this book, made more notes in my journal, and decided to set aside these thoughts temporarily. I needed to recover and spend time with my family. The end of the year was approaching, and every cell in my body longed to rest and celebrate Christmas and New Year with my loved ones.

A few days later, Hanna and I read my hospital discharge summary. We wanted to understand what had happened to me and why, at a certain point, the nurses started giving me a double dose of blood-thinning medication. On the second or third day of my hospital stay, there was a sharp spike in my D-Dimer levels in the blood test.

We began reading and delving into what D-Dimer was. I continued to receive abdominal injections after my discharge for another 20 days to lower this indicator. I recalled that the spike in the D-Dimer levels coincided with the worst days of my illness when I had a temperature of nearly 40 degrees Celsius and coughed up a basin of blood. Then, the medical staff started giving me double doses of medication in the morning and evening. I was at my worst during that period, in complete despair, saying my goodbyes to life, and that's when I turned to my parents, and the Family Channel opened.

The essence of the D-Dimer analysis is as follows: the higher this indicator, the thicker the blood in my body, and the greater the risk of blood clots forming. In such moments, there is a risk that the formed clot may detach, block a blood vessel, and result in a person's death. This is how my father passed away. The official cause of his death was a "detached clot that blocked a blood vessel in the brain." My father was gone in an instant. This is why, among other signs, I believe my father was also infected with COVID-19 in those fateful days before his death. One of the signs of COVID-19 is an elevation in the D-Dimer levels and severe blood thickening.

Hence, doctors administer abdominal injections with medication to thin the blood and prevent clot formation. Unfortunately, my father was not given this blood test and the appropriate treatment, leading to his untimely demise.

The average D-Dimer level for a healthy person my age is below 300 units. Even in pregnant women, it should not exceed 500. They started conducting this blood test on me on the first day of my hospital stay and repeated it several times a week. I entered the hospital with a D-Dimer reading already at 600. The next day, it rose to 900. And a few days later, at its peak, the test showed a value of 32,000 ! And this is not a typo ! Thirty-two thousand. My blood was as thick as jam at that moment and had difficulty flowing through the vessels. Therefore, my condition was critical.

Upon seeing the test results, Elena, Lev's godmother, and, incidentally, our family doctor said that I was fortunate to have survived. Was it luck? Now, I think not. My parents, my Family Tree, and the Universe gave me a second chance at life so that I could fulfill my purpose. This is why the revelation divided my life into "before and after."

As I see it, I turned out to be the very soul that managed to touch the Universe with the tip of my finger, comprehend its essence, and understand the meaning of Life. It's as if I were on the fresco by the great sculptor and artist Michelangelo Buonarroti, "The Creation of Adam." Perhaps the master himself experienced a moment of revelation and depicted it in this outstanding painting.

It's intriguing to think about who else in the history of humanity has encountered a phenomenon like revelation. Maybe Moses received his "Ten Commandments" through revelation? Did Newton discover the law of gravity this way? Leonardo da Vinci, Thomas Edison, Albert Einstein, who else? I wouldn't be surprised if even Nikola Tesla made his electricity-related discoveries during moments of revelation.

Perhaps Elon Musk as well? The press writes that he doesn't sleep for many hours in a row and occasionally suffers from insomnia. He constantly works on his projects. Maybe Elon Musk also received a revelation from the Universe during one of those sleepless nights? Who knows. But at least we have a chance to ask him about it. After all, he is one of the greatest minds of our time and is still planning to join Michelangelo and other geniuses of the past.

By no means do I consider myself among these geniuses. I am just an ordinary person, like most on this planet. I was fortunate enough to experience a revelation from the Universe and survive to tell you about it. And I am sure other people have experienced something similar. If you are one of them, please write to me about your experience and be sure to share your story. It will be fascinating to learn about the kernel of truth you discovered.

Returning to my revelation, the Universe's plan worked. It's as if she scattered various circumstances, knowledge, and people throughout my entire life so that in that moment of revelation, I could piece it all together bit by bit to share this information with all of humanity.

During the revelation, I assembled all the significant moments of my life into a unified picture, like a puzzle made up of a thousand pieces. I ended up in the hospital with severe COVID-19 and went through that ordeal so that the Universe, through me, could convey knowledge about the value of Life within it to everyone. My entire life's journey was a gathering of this information. The revelation resulted in the description of the Laws of the Universe and an understanding of the Universe.

I know there will be skeptics who will want to dispel my conjectures and the information I received to cast doubt on what I saw and my "touch with the Universe." It was challenging to come to terms with and believe in what was happening myself. I pondered these events and information for a whole year!

Perhaps it was medication or oxygen deficiency that caused such a state and triggered a surge in brain activity. Or there may be another explanation for my revelation. But all this is my truth, and I must live with it! I will study the workings of the human brain and find explanations for the transformations happening to me, but that will be the subject of my next book.

Right now, I am more confident than ever that I am obligated to share all this information with the world. I see this as my purpose in life. I hope you are already inspired by the ideas of the Universe's schema and are eager to learn about the "Laws of the Universe." Go for it! The next chapter is the last, but it is no less significant than all the others. It is not the endpoint of my journey or yours, but the beginning.

LAWS OF THE UNIVERSE

Finally, I would like to share my vision, understanding, and interpretation of the fundamental 'Laws of the Universe.' They were revealed to me in that very moment of revelation that changed my entire life. Since then, I have been living following these laws.

I want to introduce you to the nine fundamental Laws of the Universe that I have identified. They serve as the foundation for beginning to comprehend Life and the Universe. However, there are many other laws that humanity has already grasped and many more that we have yet to discover. Expand your understanding, and you can add new Laws of the Universe to this list that are important to you and perhaps to all of humanity.

LAW #1: OPEN MIND

"Keep your mind open; the Universe will reward you with invaluable knowledge."

A curious and open mind, filled with measures and developed comprehensively, is a priceless gift from the Universe and your diligent work! It will be your first step toward a prosperous, productive, and happy life when you realize you can learn something new. You can know anything you desire. Open your mind to further knowledge, read, explore various sources of information, analyze, draw conclusions, and the Universe will reward you with the seed of creation and encounters with the Muse.

Learn to interact with your Family Tree. Remember that Love is the key to the door of the Family Channel and connecting with the Universe. Recall departed members of your lineage more often, embrace them mentally, and express how much you love them. This will strengthen your connection with the Family Tree and the Universe.

Revelations occur only in moments of complete solitude and abstraction from the external world when your mind is clear and ready to grasp new truths. To achieve this, find a secluded place to be alone with the Universe. Learn to focus solely on your thoughts, ignoring any external distractions. And then, the Universe will surely bestow revelations upon you.

In my case, lifelong curiosity and diverse interests helped me develop my faculties so that I was fortunate enough to receive a revelation from the Universe. Now, my mind is even more open to everything and eagerly absorbs new knowledge.

LAW #2: THE UNIVERSE IS MARVELOUS

"The Universe is marvelous from every perspective."

We possess the remarkable gift of being "conscious observers." We are like the eyes of the Universe. We have the unique opportunity to see the world around us and realize that there is something greater than ourselves. Admire and relish the beauty of the Universe every second of your life! What you will see is truly marvelous!

The beauty of the Universe, its galaxies, planets, and stars will astonish your imagination. The magnificence of the Earth and all its inhabitants will not leave your heart indifferent. Your biological vessel is a perfect creation of the Universe. And your particle of Universal Energy is incredible and unique in the entire Universe.

Travel, contemplate, explore, and enjoy this Life. Visit incredible places and experience unforgettable emotions. You can find something extraordinary and exceptional in every corner of the Universe. We live a fantastic life! Trust it and the Universe! Keep your eyes and mind open!

For me, the Universe is marvelous in every aspect! I am grateful to it for allowing me to live and have my family. I rejoice like a child in the beauty of nature and the diversity of life within it. Universe, you are marvelous!

LAW #3: BE THANKFUL

"The Universe generously rewards those who sincerely express gratitude."

Sincere gratitude from the depths of your heart communicates to the Universe that you appreciate its gifts. This feedback loop is an essential tool for you and the Universe. Use it as often as you can. Then, the Universe will continue to present its gifts to you.

Gratitude will teach you to value what you already have. Without it, you may only realize the worth of something once you've lost it! There are better approaches than that. It's better to learn to appreciate what you have here and now and continue receiving new gifts rather than losing what you already have and ending up with nothing.

Thank the Universe and your Family Tree for giving your life for your beloved and close ones. Thank you for your health, a roof over your head, work, and food on the table. Be thankful for everything dear and precious to you. And the Universe will indeed bless you again.

Expressing gratitude to the Universe has become as essential as breathing air or consuming food. It's a vital ritual. It begins before sleep. I close my eyes. My thoughts turn to the Family Tree. Embracing my family tightly, I thank them for everything I have. Then, I request health and protection for my loved ones. Finally, I ask for assistance in my endeavors. This ritual is not complicated, and it's easy to repeat regularly. But it will change your entire life for the better!

LAW #4: CENTER OF THE UNIVERSE

"The Universe is boundless, and its center is within each of us."

Your Universe begins with you, your family, and your lineage. Humanity is unlikely ever to reach the boundaries of the Universe. However, I am sure that, personally for you, the center of your Universe lies within your thoughts and mind. Then, this center connects to General Universal Energy through your Family Channel.

All the events in your life, all the people you meet on your journey, and all the emotions you experience—these will determine your Universe. Undoubtedly, you are not the only living being on this planet, and your Universe will intersect with hundreds, if not thousands, of other versions of the Universe. It's essential to maintain balance, respect, and value the lives of every being.

The Universe will always be with you throughout your life. It will provide you with clues, guidance, protection, and rewards. Your task is to learn to hear and listen to the Universe, to interact with it, find your purpose, and lead a worthy, long, and happy life.

My Universe is my family! I live for them, care for them, and breathe with them. I am a part of and the center of My Universe. However, the whole world doesn't revolve around me. Earth orbits the Sun, and the Solar System revolves around the center of our galaxy, the Milky Way. And the galaxy is somewhere in the Universe. But I know for sure that my loved ones, my life experience and path, my purpose—these are the Universe in which I will live my entire life!

LAW #5: TIMELINESS

"The Universe will give you what you need when necessary."

To all your requests and prayers, the Universe always responds with "As you wish!" and bestows everything your soul desires upon you. However, don't expect results exactly when you want them. Remember that the Universe has billions of beings like you, and it takes time to shape matter, align the correct sequence of circumstances, and exert additional efforts through other living creatures. The Universe will fulfill your request and precisely provide what you desire when necessary. Just be patient and never lose faith. Keep pursuing your goals, dreaming, and thanking the Universe.

It's like listening to the orchestra of the Universe, playing a symphony in which everything is interconnected. Even if you wish to hear the first violin, which hasn't played its part yet just be patient, relax, close your eyes, and enjoy the melody. The moment you receive what you've been waiting for will come precisely when the awaited notes play.

In my life, there have been moments like this too. There were tough times when even "living from paycheck to paycheck" was challenging, and an empty wallet seemed hopeless. In moments of despair and worry about the future, the Universe sent us unexpected income, and we were "back on our feet" again.

For instance, during my revelation, while I was describing the Laws of the Universe, a moment like this occurred. The Universe made me understand that I would be in the hospital for precisely the time required for the revelation. So, this Law of "Timeliness" was the last in the list of laws, and I finished describing it the exact second the taxi stopped at the entrance of my home. It was precisely at that moment that I wrote the last word and put a period! I received all the information about the "Laws of the Universe" at a specific and definite moment. "And he went home with a clear conscience. That's how punctual our Universe is!

LAW #6: TRUST

"Just trust the Universe. You don't necessarily need to understand how everything works."

Trust in the Universe is a crucial aspect of our interaction with it. When you pray or ask the Universe for something, trust it to decide how your wish or request will be fulfilled. You don't need to know or understand how everything is structured and operates in the Universe, even though such knowledge would be a tremendous gift to humanity! Let the Universe decide how, where, and when your wish will be granted.

After all, you don't need to know all the details of how your smartphone and its programs allow you to communicate with and see your loved ones who live on the other side of the planet, do you? Just enjoy the communication and thank the Universe for this opportunity! In our childhood, we used to write letters on paper and send them in envelopes through the mail to the recipients. The letter would take days, weeks, or even months to reach its destination. It's as if your SMS or messaging app message takes a week to go in one direction and another week to return. Thanks to modern technology, we've become closer to each other, and now we can communicate at any moment without needing to know or understand how all these technologies work.

Sometimes, we receive what we desire differently from what we expect. At such times, you need to trust the Universe. It knows better what we need, as it has its plan.

A vivid example of this in my life was the purchase of an apartment in a new building in Kyiv. My wife, Hanna, and I struggled to find a good offer for a long time. Finding the right construction site and a reliable developer took time. Like hotcakes, the "perfect" apartments were snatched right before us. Among all the available options on the market, only one bank offered reasonable conditions that suited us. Finally, we found our dream apartment and applied for a mortgage. Imagine our disappointment when our application was denied. Our dream apartment turned into a pumpkin. It felt as if the whole world was against us! It was as if the Universe was saying, "You don't need this," and we weren't listening to its hints, insisting on our way.

And then, one day, out of the blue, the bank called me and said they had approved a mortgage for a lower amount and had a couple of apartment options in an excellent building. My feet carried me to the bank in a matter of minutes, across the city. In the blink of an eye, I chose a floor plan and signed the contract. Hooray! We became owners of a magnificent apartment in the capital! Everything went smoothly as if it was meant to be at the right moment and place.

For a whole year, while our building was under construction, Hanna and I dreamed of how we would live in our new apartment. We mentally decorated and furnished it. Every time we walked with our daughter, we visited our construction site and eagerly anticipated the long-awaited move-in moment. And then, after a year... the construction was frozen. After a couple of years of unsuccessful battles with the bank and city authorities, our bank closed, transferring the problematic project to another developer. "How could this happen, Universe?! This was supposed to be our nest! We've worked so hard for this, and we lost it so quickly!". It was a low blow. This bitter disappointment in the impotence of authorities, a corruption-laden scheme, and the vulnerability of ordinary citizens became my final straw. It prompted me to decide to move to Poland.

A year and a half later, on February 24, 2022, a full-scale war broke out in Ukraine. The brutal invasion of a neighboring state into our territory spilled blood and killed thousands of innocent people. The proximity of war made me consider yet another migration, as far away as possible from everything happening. That's how we ended up in Canada, and we've been living here for a year now. And what about our apartment? The unfinished building still stands. And I continue to pay off the mortgage for a beautifully stacked pile of bricks.

The situation with the apartment didn't turn out the best for me, but I trusted the Universe! It must have been meant to be. This unfinished project came into my life so that I could move to another country and provide my family with a more stable and secure life. If the building had been completed and we had moved into our apartment, we would now live there with regular power outages, water shortages, and heating problems, under constant rocket attacks, and trembling with fear for our lives. Thank you, Universe, for this important lesson! And for the fact that thanks to this apartment, my family is now safe in Canada. I can thank you for publishing this book.

LAW #7: SENSE OF HUMOR

"The Universe has an excellent sense of humor: witty, refined, and sharp."

A sense of humor is the ability of a person to acquire and convey a positive energy, creating moments of happiness. It's a way for the Universe to multiply energy. A sense of humor helps one endure tough times and overcome despair, fear, anger, and horror. It's a way to "lighten the mood."

The Universe has its unique sense of humor. It's refined, witty, and has a twist. These qualities manifest themselves in how you achieve the desired result. You will sometimes get what you want as you envisioned it. As you may recall, the Universe has billions of people like you; conducting them all is more complex. But you will definitely get what you want if you set goals correctly and make efforts to achieve them. And when the moment of reward comes, the Universe may display its sense of humor and play out the situation in a way you didn't expect, leaving you with a positive impression.

Learn to recognize the subtle thread of Universal humor, and you will appreciate its wit. This skill didn't come to me immediately, but I noticed situations where traces of Universal spirit were evident over time. It helped me not give up in difficult situations, smooth out sharp corners, and reduce tension.

Develop a sense of humor within yourself. Bring positivity to your environment and charge everyone with your energy! And remember to thank the Universe for its sense of humor.

LAW #8: BALANCE

"The Universe seeks harmony and balance of energy."

The Universe's inclination toward harmony, balancing positive and negative energy, is inherent in the very nature of Life. After all, if you only have positive energy, the world will cease to evolve and develop. You can't build a new house on old ruins. You can only create a society close to perfection by breaking old norms. You can't gain new knowledge if you're sure you already possess it and don't doubt its truth.

The same is true about negative energy. If you only, have it, life will self-destruct to its core and possibly come to an end. Destructive energy can destroy everything: your body, family, humanity, and Life. That's why there will always be a harmonious tandem of positive and negative energies to allow Life in the Universe to evolve.

The current war in Ukraine is terrifying and bloody. Every day, I thank the Universe for the fact that my family, friends, and loved ones are alive, healthy, and relatively safe. I sincerely believe and wish for Ukraine to emerge victorious in this fierce battle against total evil and the absence of humanity!

But with time came the understanding that it's worth trusting the Universe. There may be no other option. Without these awful events, there would be no chance to break old norms, dismantle outdated systems, and rid humanity of the relics of the past legacy. In one way or another, this destructive force will become the foundation for constructive energy, and we will enter a new era of prosperity and harmony! The world will shake off the ashes, heal its wounds, regain strength, and boldly step into a new, happy, bright future! And Ukraine will bloom again and sing like never before with the song of a nightingale! The Universe always knows what's best. So, let's trust it and its sense of balance.

LAW #9: LIFE

"Your life is a Wonder in the Universe!"

Life is a unique phenomenon in the Universe. Your specific life is as significant as the existence of Life as a whole. Embrace it as a gift and live it with dignity. You have only one life; cherish it.

From the moment of your birth, when the Spark of Life ignites, until the moment it fades away, you have a unique and incredible gift – your Life. It will be magnificent! It is filled with bright emotions, exciting people, and fascinating events. The astonishing beauty of the Universe will mesmerize you; keep your eyes, heart, and mind wide open and explore the world around you. Find your kindred souls while you can. They will fill your life with Love! Live, enjoy, and be happy!

I've learned to cherish every moment of my life, and every moment spent with family, friends, and like-minded people. Every second that makes me happy. I rejoice in everything new like a child. I savor the bright flavors and scents that each new day brings. I dream every day of doing something significant for the world and the Universe. I strive to become even happier and want to live a long life filled with unforgettable experiences! Because it's mine! Only I can fill it with love and happiness and create a Wonder! Because I am a "Wonder in the Universe"! And so are you!

EPILOGUE

"It's not too late to stop. To reconsider.
And to make everything right.

Before we destroy Life itself. Completely and forever..."

In conclusion, I would like to share more thoughts with you. I believe it's time to eradicate the "divide and conquer" ideology from our society. It may benefit many nations, those in power, religions, and some individuals, but it is destructive. What has it led to? Humanity is divided into ideological groups that constantly conflict with one another. We must learn to live peacefully with our neighbors and cooperate to achieve more significant results. Not to mention the millennia of wars between tribes, nations, and states. Have we remained "unfriendly neighbors" after thousands of years? Has humanity yet to progress and evolve?

I propose implementing a new ideology – "unite and thrive"! Why do family values matter so much to me personally? Hanna and

I "united" to "thrive" as a family: looking in the same direction, facing difficulties on our path to success, having children, taking care of our family, and helping each other in everyday tasks. This has been my core ideology for many years, and it works! So why not project it onto all of humanity's areas of our lives?

Imagine the world we could create if we stopped fighting for territories, resources, and religions. It sounds like a utopia, but isn't it worth striving for perfection instead of degradation? Haven't millennia of wars proven that it's a path to nowhere? War only brings destruction, death, hatred, and discord for future generations!

It's time for humanity to realize that Earth is round and there is nowhere else to escape. We have no other home or territory for our species and all living beings to survive. History has shown that conquering the entire planet is impossible! No one has even conquered a whole continent yet. So why start wars again and again? The unity of nations in organizations, alliances, and unions yields results. Yes, it's more complicated than it seems at first glance. But the direction is right, bringing together people of different nationalities, faiths, and political beliefs under one roof.

Caring for others is the path to civilization's development while caring only for oneself is its decline. Selfishness is humanity's enemy. If we think more about and care for others than ourselves, there will be fewer problems.

The same goes for "religious wars." How many religions exist in the world today? It's an enormous number that's difficult to count.

Does this mean there are just as many deities that people believe in or even more? Is it possible that each of these gods created their world, but we all live in them simultaneously? Does one God die and another is born when you change your religion? These conflicting ideas have no end.

The abundance of religions is due to the same processes that created many states. Different nations developed their customs and cultures, creating their gods. But if you look closely, remove the noise, the religious attributes, and divine images, you'll see that humanity believes in "something greater than ourselves, some force or super mind that created everything around us gave us life, and governs all of this." Any measure can symbolize this concept, but the essence remains the same. I've chosen the Universe as my measure. It's my God if you will. And all of humanity is under its protection.

Isn't it time for us to unite our beliefs? Because each of them contains so much good, beauty, and inspiration! We must take the best from each religion and create one perfect one. Uniting all people under one "faith" will end "religious wars" and conflicts.

I realize that there may never be an ideal society. The Universe will always seek balance and harmony between positive and negative energies. There will likely still be room for conflicts, disagreements, and arguments. But we must learn to be restrained, to exit rows gracefully, and to find compromises. We are endowed with the priceless gift of controlling our lives! This allows us to choose our path, make decisions, and take responsibility for the consequences. We can and must create that "Perfect World."

All conflicts arose from a lack of understanding of one another because we defined the world around us with different measures. Each nation lived on its territory and built its families, tribes, and communities. At that time, defending oneself and responding to "foreigners" who came to their land with war was natural. But today, in the modern world of technology, accessible information, extensive migration processes, and the mixing of different peoples in one territory, hasn't it become clear that humanity is a single species, Homo sapiens? And we all live together on one planet, Earth. We must find ways to unite and thrive together!

How many countries do you know today where the population consists of 100% indigenous people? Especially if you look not at their passports but at the genetic makeup of everyone. I don't know of any. But there isn't a single isolated state left.

Not to mention families whose genetic makeup is a mix of different races. I have Ukrainian and Russian blood flowing in my veins, and maybe something else, but I don't know. My mother was from Ukraine, and my father was from Russia. I was born in Ukraine and spent most of my life there. I am Ukrainian by nationality, but I can't change my genetic heritage. In these challenging times for Ukraine, my heart breaks into pieces because parts of my family are on opposite sides of the barricades, and I love them all equally. Due to the ambitions and recklessness of those in power who started this war, millions of innocent people suffer.

If you think are only of one race, take a DNA test and explore your genetic makeup. I'm sure you'll be pleasantly surprised!

If there is no single nation with only one non-mixed gene, and there are more and more people with a mixed gene pool, why has not everyone realized and accepted the truth that we are all one biological species and live with the same basic needs, processes and values? So, why not unite as one large "family" and resolve conflicts with reason rather than force? Just imagine the prosperity humanity could achieve if we stopped squandering insane budgets on weaponry and wars and redirected them toward constructive endeavors.

Do we have other problems and challenges to confront? Climate change and catastrophes, hunger and overconsumption of resources, epidemics and viral infections, carbon emissions into the atmosphere, economic and political crises, incurable human diseases, numerous divorces and the breakdown of the family institution, interpersonal conflicts, and so on. This list could go on indefinitely. This is what humanity should be combating, not each other. This list of "common human enemies" can help us all unite and become one species, one large family living on Earth in the Universe.

As a bloody war rages in Ukraine, and humanity stands on the brink of a third World War, possibly a nuclear war, one begins to realize the fragility and value of human life and life on Earth. We still need to find out if life exists elsewhere. Perhaps we are the only representatives of life in the Universe. If there is another Life somewhere, it's likely different from ours, with its unique forms. Earthly life is fantastic throughout the Universe!

If life only exists on Earth, we should learn to cherish and value it in all its manifestations. Suppose we sever the connection of Universal Energy with matter and break the thread of all Life by destroying humanity and all living things on this planet. In that case, the Universe cannot be guaranteed to restore Life. And if it can, it will once again require billions of years to evolve into a life form close to that of humans. We must not allow this under any circumstances!

My purpose is to convey to humanity the idea of the value and fragility of Life in all its forms and manifestations in the Universe. And the importance of human life as the pinnacle of evolutionary intelligence.

I hope this idea will help everyone realize that humanity, as a biological species, must cease killing one another and, at any cost, prevent the impending third world war. A nuclear war that would be the last for all of humanity and possibly for all of Life. I hope we still have time and can redirect the vector of humanity's self-destruction in the opposite direction.

The critical thought for me became the phrase received during my revelation:

"It's not too late to stop. To reconsider. And to make everything right. Before we destroy Life itself. Completely and forever..."

Now you know what a "Wonder in the Universe" is – Life in any form and manifestation. The delicate thread of Universal Energy fills different biological vessels, infusing them with Life. It's the Wonder within every living being and each of us, in me and you. You and I are unique fragments of Life in the Universe. But together, we are Life itself! Life is you! You are the Wonder!

Our primary task is to protect this Wonder. We must preserve Life in the Universe in all its forms and manifestations. Just think, the Universe created the world we call home through billions of years of evolution! Today, humanity, which considers itself the pinnacle of evolution, can instantly destroy all the Universe's efforts. We are obligated to preserve Life at all costs!

This book has given you only a tiny piece of knowledge and understanding of the Universe's structure, our place in it, and our interaction with it. Everything you need to know about the Universe is within it. Just choose the proper measures. Keep exploring the Universe, for it is magnificent!

Now you know "who you are and why you came into this world." You are a part of Universal Energy that needs to live your unique and happy life, full of discoveries and accomplishments, among loving souls.

So, what should you do with your Wonder in the Universe, your life?

1. *Enjoy every second of your life.*
2. *Take care of your biological shell to live as long as possible.*
3. *To multiply Universal positive energy, Experience as many happy moments as possible.*
4. *Find your kindred souls. Love and be loved.*
5. *Build a family, have children, frequently tell them how much you love them, and cherish moments with them.*
6. *Every day, connect with your Family Tree, remembering your ancestors so their memory helps the Tree live forever.*
7. *Keep your mind open to everything new and your soul open to Love.*
8. *Explore new measures and transition to new stages of brain development.*
9. *Identify and fulfill your gifts and talents.*
10. *Find your purpose and fulfill it.*
11. *Savor every bit of our marvelous Universe.*
12. *Change the world for the better!*
13. *Thank the Universe!*

In the world, there are numerous nations, states, and religions. Each has its measures and understanding of the structure and processes in the Universe. Humanity has devised many measures to describe how the Universe is organized and our place within it. The diversity of languages and cultural heritages, the multitude of religions and faiths, and various sciences – people like you and I created all these.

Someone spoke the first word; someone wrote the Ten Commandments; someone described the laws of physics. It wasn't Gods but wise individuals who documented everything around us. Everything you read, know, and use every day – people created all of it. It was their vision, understanding, and realization. These measures may differ, but they allow us to obtain and comprehend information about the matter around us. Perhaps these measures are imperfect, but they are necessary for absolute understanding of the Universe!

On the pages of this book, I have offered you my measure, experience, vision, and understanding of the Universe. This measure is based on existing human knowledge, with the addition of my own experience and perception of what is happening around us. Undoubtedly, there are differences and disagreements with other measures, and I certainly do not claim absolute truth. My task was to pass on knowledge to my children and their descendants and help them live a long, happy life filled with love! As for which measure resonates with you the most, that's for you to decide. Remember, you were born with the right to choose how to live your life! This is your Life; enjoy it every second!

I hope you have found a lot of valuable information for yourself within the pages of my book. If you contemplate your existence, discover your purpose in life, and become happier, then I have fulfilled my mission. Come back periodically and reread the pages of this book, "Wonder in the Universe." Be inspired, delve deeper into the essence of knowledge, and draw strength from positive energy. And remember to thank the Universe for everything!

As for me, I will go on living my exciting and happy life surrounded by loved ones, never forgetting to continue developing my measure further, in the hopes of one day meeting you again on the pages of a new book.

Thank you for making this book a part of your life. With the deepest gratitude,

Alex Chudov

THANK YOU, MY DEAR READER!

THANK YOU, THE UNIVERSE!

www.ingramcontent.com/pod-product-compliance
Lightning Source LLC
Chambersburg PA
CBHW071605030726
47593CB00001BA/325
9781069154514